EUGENIO PUCCI

VENICE

A Complete Guide for Visiting the City

BONECHI   EDITIONS « IL TURISMO »
Via dei Rustici, 5 - FLORENCE

«MERCURIO» SERIES
OF BONECHI GUIDE

Translated by
LOUIS GIARDINI

Have a happy stay in Venice

Addressing myself to the tourist, from whatever part of the world he may come, I should like to offer, almost affectionately, and with all my heart, welcome to this incomparable many-faceted city. To satisfy his desire to see everything and know everything, usually in the shortest time possible and with the most reasonable expense, I feel I can offer my « Guide of Venice », which has been compiled with a sense of love by Eugenio Pucci — a Florentine in love with Venice — a writer used to the many things of beauty in his Florence, who in my opinion is in a position to see and understand Venice, from his numerous visits to this splendid city of which he has captured not only the fundamental elements but also the minor ones, either from the historical or the artistic point of view.

So this guide, within certain limits imposed by practical and economic reasons, can be considered by the visitor as an indispensable friend for its completeness. You will find in it a Venice illustrated in her manifold aspects: from the original formation as a city to the confirmation of her maritime and commercial power; from the characteristic innermost aspects to the brilliance of her incomparable natural and artistic beauties. We have aimed at clarity, not omitting the necessary aesthetic notes which are so indispensable for the majority of visitors, for whom the pace of life today is such that it has not permitted a more profound study of the subject. Because it is easy in a city like Venice to lose one's way, I also recommend the use of the extensive alphabetical index and the clear plan of the city.

Being certain, without presumption, of having produced something useful and of value, may I again offer a warm welcome, and wish you a very happy stay in this charming and evocative city.

THE EDITOR

INDEX

Museums, Galleries, Churches, Palaces,
Monuments, etc.

HISTORICAL BACKGROUND

FORMATION OF THE CITY:

First of all the name. Why Venice? The origin of this name goes back to the time when an Indo-European population different from the Italic settled in the Venetian plains.
This happened in the second millennium B.C., and, very probably, this population came from Illyria. These people subjugated the Euganei, founded Vicenza, Treviso, Padua, Este, Belluno and other cities. In the first century B.C. these cities were latinized by the Roman conquest, and, from this period, the people were called *Venetians*. The word *Venetians*, il truly of Indo-European origin, would assume the meaning of « noblemen »; if, on the other hand, it is pre-Indo-European, its meaning would be « foreigners » or « newcomers ». It is to be presumed, therefore, that from newcomers has derived the ord *Venetians*, and, from Venetians to Venice, the difference is obvious.

The growth of Venice represents a very complex process hich has taken place through many centuries. The nucleus of the city took place in the zone of Rialto. Canals were built and the earth obtained thereof was used to raise and to reinforce the fabricated area. Thus originated the Grand Canal and the numerous brooks (rii) of the city which connect today over 118 little islands through more than 400 bridges. These islands were made stronger by a tight disposition of tree trunks on which are built the foundations of the houses and of the palaces. The urban conglomeration from West to East is 4260 meters long, and, from North to South, 2790 meters wide. It covers an area of 7,062 square kilometers. The perimeter of the city, including the islands of the Maritime Station, of Saint George, of Saint Helen, and the Giudecca is 13,700 kilometers.

On account of its topographical configuration, Venice appears to the visitor as a city of dreams, springing from the waters luminous and splendid which reveals a different language each season through its endless merits: historical places, natural beauties, art the traditional hospitality and kindness of its people contribute to the uniqueness of this city. The very famous Grand Canal, or Canalazzo, as it is called by the natives, with its marvelous sequence of beautiful palaces and picturesque houses, is the main artery of the city. It is shaped like an «S» turned upside down, it is 3,8000 meters long and, at some points 30 and in others 70 meters wide; its depth is from five to five and a half meters. The canal divides the city into two parts and flows into the bigger Saint Mark's Canal in the waters of which shines the imposing Ducal Palace. This big artery, through three bridges (that of the railway station, that of Rialto and that of the Academy) and forty-five brooks that flow into it, allow easy communication with all the « sestieri » (zones) of the city.

The characteristic «rii» or «rielli» are about four to five meters wide and can only be used by gondolas. By these «rii» are the roads, often small and twisted, which are called «calli». These lead into open spaces that are called «campi» if the area is quite big, and «campielli» if it is of small dimensions. The «rii» can also lead into the «corti», so called on account of their dead ends. The names of the sestieri into which the city is divided are the following: Saint Mark, Castello, Cannareggio, Saint Croce, Saint Paul and Sorsoduro which also includes the parish of Saint Eufemia alla Giudecca. In these sestieri live a population of over two hundred thousand people. Venice is connected with land and is four kilometers distant from it. Besides the several maritime

Historical Regatta along the Grand Canal.

services, two bridges on the laguna complete the network: the railroad bridge was built in 1841-46, it is 3,601 meters long; the road bridge was built in 1931-32, it is 4,070 meters long, and 20 meters wide. For a good part the two bridges run together.

THE CLIMATE:
Venice is fortunate to have a very moderate climate. As a matter of fact the average yearly temperature is 14°,4 centigrades; winter is rarely very cold, and summer is not too warm; there is abundant rainfall from summer to autumn. As far as wind is concerned, the city is more frequently hit by the North-East wind (from Greece) which is especially felt during the month of May. A peculiar aspect assumes the city during the so-called high tide, or, « high water », as the Venetians call the swelling of the sea which obeys the attracting force of the sun and of the moon. As a rule the waters invade the square of Saint Mark and reach a height of over ½ meter; the gondolas can well travel on this sea on the square, and the inhabitants must use anything that floats to reach one point of the invaded area. These inondations are the cause of the slow erosion of the foundations of the various public and private buildings.

THE PATRON, THE PIGEONS, AND THE GONDOLAS:

Venice has had two Patron Saints: San Todaro (Theodore), of Greek origin, represented at the beginning of the formation of the Republic his lovalty to the Byzantine Empire; the second Patron is San Marco Evangelista whose body was brought to Venice in 828 by two Venetians merchants in order to remove it from the profanation of the Moslems. The Patron was thus transported from the church in Alexandria, Egypt, in which the Evangelist underwent martyrdom at the period of Napolen, to Venice.

The sacred relics was solemnly accepted and the Saint declared the effective Patron of the city. As the symbol of this Evangelist is a winged lion, it was adopted as the coat-of-arms of the city.

But Venice also has another attribute; namely, that of «Serenissima» (most serene) because of the fact that the Government followed in all its social and political actions a serene concept of justice. Its high magistracies, not being tied to any factions or parties, were in the position of passing judgment on every topic of pubblic interest with the greatest serenity. It is for this reason that we see the Republic depicted with symbols of justice: the sword and the scale.

Tourists are immediately received by the festive flights of pigeons upon arriving in Piazza San Marco. According to an old legend, they were brought from Ciprius to Venice as a gift to the wife of the Doge. The pigeons are considered by Venetians a tradition and ornament of the city; they are cared for by the city. City Hall sees to it that they receive an abundant ratio of corn at nine A.M. and at one P.M. During the tourist season this allowance is greatly increased as a very great number of visitors hold out their hands and feed the pigeons in order to be photographed in a multi-colored cloud of wings. But, besides pigeons, tourists are attracted by the gondolas that slide elegantly, silently and romantically along the waters of the Canal Grande or the numerous «rii» and reminding them of the romances of the past as in a dream... and, why not?, of the presente also. And, since we are talking about gondolas, let us see the derivation of this word. According to the « Venetian Lexicon » by Mutinelli, this name derives from cymbula, a little boat. As, in former times, «y» was pronunced «u», and often «c» was pronunced «g» by the Venetians, the word «gundula» (later gondola) was born. The gondola is a small row boat with a flat bottom and measuring four or five meters in length and one meter and fifty in width, it is ornamented with a sort of covered little room with small windows at the sides, a really ideal place for the «innamorati» (lovers).

Nocturnal view of Piazza San Marco and the Ducal Palace.

THE HYSTORY OF THE CITY

FROM THE V CENTURY TO THE YEAR 1200:

There have been two reasons for the formation of the Republic of Venice: the fall of the Roman Empire of the West and the invasions of the barbarians.

The inhabitants of those Venetians cities, hit by the passage of the armies of Attila, Alaricus, Theodoricus, and Alboinus sought to escape to the lagoons and occupied the small islands which were for the most part inhabited by sailors, swamp hunters and salt workers.

Thus, the exiled ones from Aquileia, Altino, Caorle took refuge in Grado, Torcello, Concordia: those in Monselice and Paua settled for good in Iesolo, Murano, Mazzorbo and Mamamoco. As we can see, it was a considerable sojourn; so much so, that it allows to fix the the year 451 as the probable date of the foundation of the city.

Of course the new inhabitants of the Venetian laguna gave themselves a political and social code with the bringing into being of the «Maritime Tribunes» who were appointed by the viceroy of Ravenna (the exarch), a representative of the Western Roman Empire which had its capital in Bisantium. Thus the new state is born under the direct dependence of this city which in the VII century, when the Venetians abolished the government of the

«Maritime Tribunes» and decided on the election of a Duke or Doge, approves the change thus making the first Doges imperially appointed. When, however, difficulties of a religious nature, came up between the Byzantine Empire and the Papacy, the Venetians slowly relinquished Byzantine authority and inserted themselves into the Italian political realities. From this moment on the Doges are elected by the Popular Assembly.

The formation of the new state brought about internal dissents over the assignment of public positions. These internal fights ended, however, with the need of stopping Pepin, the King of the Franks, from the conquest of the Venetian lagoon. When a naval fleet came before « Civitas Rivoalti », it was blocked by the sands and easily defeated by the Venetians. In 812 the peace of Acquisgrana between the Western Empire and the Carolingians confirmed the dependence of Venice on Bisantium. This allowed Venice to concentrate on her preparation as a maritime power so that in a very short time she became the link between West and East. It was in this way that Venice in the IX century, by means of arms and diplomacy, was able to become the master of the Istrian, Dalmatian and Pugliese coasts under one of her greatest Doges: Pietro Orseolo II. In the XI century Bisantium had to face the Normans who, after the conquest of the Pugliese coasts, aimed at becoming bosses of Albania. The Byzantine emperor invited Venice to block the way to the Normans. She intervened, and, from the common victory, she gained incalculable political and economical benefits; thus becoming more than a satellite but an ally of the Byzantine Empire.

Quite fortunate in maritime and commercial undertakings, Venice kept an eye open on what was taking place on the terra firma and, from the struggles between the Comunes and the Empire, she knew how to get benefits for her work as a mediator and a safekeeper of her own interests. Venice's very able statesmanship achieved in 1177 the reconciliation between Emperor Frederic Barbarossa and Pope Alexander III.

This is the famous reconciliation which took place in Venice in the Basilica of Saint Mark and which saw Barbarossa prostrated before the Roman Pontiff. Yet, in order to consolidate the success obtained outside the country, the Venetians had to reinforce their own institutions as a result of the attempt of various Doges to transform the Dogado into a hereditary monarchy. Thus, in 1032, an appropriate constitutional law was passed which prohibited the Doge to exercise power through his relatives.

At this stage the Republic looks with a certain diffidence to the initiative of Pope Urban II who launches a crusade of Italian and foreign princes for the recovery of the holy places in Jerusalem. The situation was becoming delicate on account of the commercial traffic with the East and the political action that was being developed by the various powers in that sector. Venice kept thus the position of careful and patient observer, but it was not lacking in sensitivity when Pope Innocent III launched the fourth crusade. The doge at that time was eighty-year-old Enrico Dandolo who can be defined the real founder of the economic and military power of the « Serenissima ». He acted in such a way as to get the best of the situation; he supplied free ships and equipment to the Crusaders, and, in return, with their help, he conquered Zara in 1202. During this contingency the people of Costantinople deposed its Monarch Alessio who asked the Crusaders for help. The Doge intuited soon the importance of his intervent and caused the weapons of the crusades to change route and go to Constantinople. The undertaking was successful

A characteristic waterway.

but the people revolted against Alessio and the Crusaders had to fight in order to take again the city. The princes of the crusades divided among themselves the rich lands of Bisantium and Venice got the lion's share by taking « over one quarter of the Empire ». From this we can understand how wide was becoming the economic influence of Venice in the East. Her merchant ships docked at all harbors in the Adriatic, in the Aegean, in the Dardanelles, at the sea of Marmora, of Egypt and Asia Minor. Marco Polo went as far as China. From the rich colonies and from visits at the above-named ports of calls, the ships came home loaded with the most precious things and of materials for artistic works: which permitted to the Republic to sell to all of Europe her manufactured goods and to invest her capital in very rewarding commercial undertakings.

So much economic prosperity also caused a radical constitutional reform which allowed the Republic to keep her role as a great power for a long time. The reforms happened little by little. At the beginning of the XI century public finances were administered by the procurators of Saint Mark instead of the Doge. In 1172 was instituted the Major Council whose members (480) were elected by a well-thought-of electoral law which gave prevalence to the noble classes. In 1178 was established the Little Council which increased membership from two to six; the following year is established the Supreme Tribunal of the Quarantia, a sort of Senate composed of forty members which constituted the highest magistrature of the Republic; then, the so-called «pregadi» were created; namely, the most influential citizens called to give advice to the Doge for the good functioning of public institutions. In 1297 a reunion of the Mayor Council caused new legislative dispositions to insure to the Patrician classes access to public positions and to the Dogeship. These series of reforms were the cause of bitter fights among various sects of the citizenry. To be remembered is the Querini-Tiepolo plot in 1300 which was resolved with the exile of the latter, but which also caused the institution of the famous Council of the Ten, for the security of the State. This council became so powerful as to decree the death sentence to Doge Marin Faliero for betraying public instituions because he attempted to become the absolute Lord of the Republic.

FROM 1200 TO 1500
But things don't go always well for the Republic. Another maritime power contends her commercial leadership in the Mediterranean: the Republic of Genoa. This city engaged her rival in a hard and long war which lasted almost one century. At first Genoa supports Michael the Paleologist in his revenges towards the Byzantine throne, obtaining in return so many privileges that he became a real danger to Venetian traffics. Then followed the difficult contests which caused a sequence of defeats and victories. Thus Venice had to face the battles of Curzola, Alghero, Anzio, Zara until the last episode of the siege of Chioggia in which Venetian arms, led by Vettor Pisani, reported a decisive victory which permitted to the Republic to reconquer her lost positions. Thus at the beginning of the sixteenth century she is once again one of the strongest and most to-be-feared powers in Europe.

Powerful at sea and secure from any surprise on this side, the Republic of Saint Mark feels the need to protect herself at the shoulders; namely, from the terra firma. It was necessary to have under her all the zone of the Marca Trevigiana, Feltre, Bassano, Padua, and Verona. She knew how to conquer these places with political ability and military capacity. The dispossessed Lords; namely, the Scaligeri and the Carrarese sent against Venice the armies of King Sigismondo, but even he was defeated and had to concede Friuli and Udine. Venice's fortunes inland

A picturesque view of Venice at sunset.

caused other near-by cities to reflect. These cities, such as Vicenza, asked to belong to the Republic of Venice. The expansion of the Serenissima arose the suspicion of Filippo Maria Visconti, the Duke of Milan, who sought to control her expansion by force. Thus ensued a long struggle which saw the very capable Doge Francesco Foscari engaged against the Milanese State which was defeated and which had to give away in the Peace Treaty of Cremona in 1441, Peschiera, Brescia and Bergamo. Shortly afterwards, upon the death of the Duke of Milano, Venice came into possession of Ravenna di Lodi and of Piacenza; but the war continues with Francesco Sforza. But, even the latter comes to terms with the peace of Lodi in 1454, at which time the border of Adda was recognized to the Venetian Republic. It was, thus, an enviable situation for the Serenissima; which, from this moment on, together with Florence and Milano, is one of the main factors for the economic and political stability in Italy.

Venice had thus reached the apex of her grandeur and power. However, the historical events which took place in the fifteenth and sixteenth centuries were such that caused the beginning of the ennemy was completely destroyed. The Turks took was given by the Turks who in the past held with Venice amicable relations both on the political and economic level. This frendship ended, however, in 1416 when the Mussulmans, with a sudden move, invaded and raped the islands of Euboea and Cicladi. Venice intervened and in a memorable battle Doge Pietro Loredan inflicted to them such a hard blow that the fleet of the ennemy was completely destroyed. The Turks took once more the initiative and conquered Tessalonica; thus putting before the Venetians the alternative of a declaration of war. They preferred to reach an agreement with Mohammed II in return for economic benefits; however, the Mussulman leader had great ambitions and did not observe the agreements and started again the war which brough him the Dukedom of Athens, of Morea and during a decennium, despite sporadic successes of the Venetians, he gained control of Argus and Negropont. The situation became truly dangerous for the Serenissima which saw herself menaced in her own territory, and, once again, she preferred coming to an agreement by renouncing to her possessions and pledging to pay a huge annual toll in order to keep the possibility of carrying on commerce in the territories of Mezzaluna. At this demonstration of retreat, the Turks understood that Venetian power was declining. Thus hostilities started again a little later and other territories were taken from the Adriatic Republic, despite the great naval battle of 1499 in Navarrino which had a negative outcome for both parties concerned.

FROM 1500 TO 1866:

Always on account of the Turkish threat, Venice lost Modone, Corone and Lepanto. She was thus once again compelled into signing a peace treaty in 1503 which mutilated her of a great portion of the territory of Morea. The series of misfortunes continues with the war of 1537-40 which sees the defeat of the Venetian naval fleet at Prevesa. Yet, she was soon consoled with the purchase of Cyprus as a result of the wedding of King Giacomo II di Lusignano with the beautiful Venetian Patrician Catharine Corner. Cyprus, with Famagosta as its capital, became a powerful bulwark for defending the interests of the Venetians; yet, even this one fell in 1570 into the hands of the Turks despite bold deeds by the defensors under the leadership of the heroic Marcantonio Bragadin. The strenuous resistance opposed to the invaders, which caused great losses to them, was the reason for the pityless Mussulman vengeance: the massacre of the ennemy and the skinning alive of the bold leader.

The very serious Venetian defeat and the ferocious Turkish vengeance opened the eyes of those responsible statesmen who, in turn, decided to put an end to the Mussulman expansion. After recovery, Venice, together with Spain, the Savoias, and the Knights from Malta, faces the big fleet of the adversary at Lepanto in 1571 and caused great losses and escape to the ennemy. However, such great victory did not bring Venice any benefit because a great portion of the Turkish fleet was able to escape, Spain left the League and the Serenissima was again pressured into an uneasy peace treaty in which she had to renounce to Cyprus and other possessions.

As we have seen above, the first cause for the decadence of Venice has been the struggle against the Turks who little by little have dragged away from her territories and positions of privilege; the second, and more important, cause for Venetian decline have been the geographical discoveries which took place at the end of the XV century. It was the Potuguese who passing from Cape of Good Hope, determined commercial contacts with the Indies.

At one time all goods and raw materials had to go through the Red Sea and Egypt. From here, on Venetian ships, they arrived in Europe. The fact that European powers could make use of the new commercial route took away from Venice her supremacy in this field. This was a great blow to Venice, and, in order to recover from it, she proposed in 1504 to the Egyptian Sovereign the opening of the opening of the Suez Isthmus. Unfortunately, the idea could not be carried out.

From this moment one can say that Venice had to face her economic needs with her immense accumulated wealth and with an alert commercial politics, towards European countries.

To the battle of Lepanto followed a long peace, but the Turks awaked again in 1644 and took possession of the island of Crete, the last Venetian possession in the Eastern portion of the Mediterranean. The following year it was the turn of the island of Candia and the Republic had to wage a war for twenty-five years during which she reported brilliant successes, but was unable to prevent the fall of Candia which was defended with great heroism. As a matter of fact the island capitulated on the 5 of September, 1669, and to its defensors the ennemy conceded the honor of the weapons. However, the Mussulman undertaking had to present to Venice an opportunity of a return match; in fact the Turks had gone as far as Vienna and besieged her. The Republic put itself at the head of the Holy Alliance constituted by Europeans, and gave the command of the fleet to the heroic defensor of Candia, Francesco Morosini. This man, after a ten-year war, was capable of bringing back to his country Morea and other eminent positions of privilege which were confirmed at the peace of Carlowitz in 1699. Thus started a period of tranquillity.

Not less unfortunate have been Venice's diplomatic and military experiences in terra firma from 1467 to 1516. Many were the quarrels and, at a certain point, Venice found herself against all the small Italian states and the great European powers envious of her prosperity and prestige. This happened against the famous League of Cambray.

The war had many alternate events and(after the defeat of Agnadello, Venice lost almost the whole terra firma, but did not give up. In 1510 she succeeded in defeating the allies and with the peace of Noyon she got back everything she had lost. After these severe trials, the Serenissima went ahead with much caution but never practiced political renunciation. France and Austria had to recognize her control of the Adriatic and the border of the Adda border; in the period 1613-20 she was able to prevent a conspiracy which, if successful, would have made her a subject of the Austrian Empire. By this time, though, Venice was exhausted; she did not even participate to the wars of succession between Spain, Poland and Austria and had her territory invaded by the armies of the contendants. Between 1766 and 1792 she still had a few initiatives to fight against pirate ships which disturbed the commercial traffic in the Mediterranean.

To speed up the fall of the Republic, by now even economically beat, intervened the French Revolutionary Movement with its new social ideas which are in apparent contrast with the old, aristocratic, Venetian constitution. Napoleon will finish Venice when, in May 1, 1797, he conquered the Veneto territory and asked for the abolition of the constitution in order to nominate a popular government, but then, in October of the same year, the destiny of Venice was decided with the treaty of Campoformio: she will become the slave of Austria. But this slavery the Venetians will know how to abolish in 1848-49 by participating to the popular movements for the First Unity of Italy led by Daniele Manin. The heroic and unfortunate Venetians gave in only on account of hunger and cholera. They saw the return of the Austrians who stayed there until 1866, the year in which the Venetians, because of the defeat of the Austrian-Prussian armies by the young Kingdom of Italy and of the French, decreed the union of Italy with a triumphal plebiscite of 674,426 «yes» against 69 «no».

ARTISTIC BACKGROUND

ARCHITECTURAL STYLES: A visit to Venice will reveal to us four architectural styles each of which is typical of an epoch. We have the Byzantine, the Romanesque, the Gothic, and the Renaissance styles.

Here are their particular structure. The *Byzantine style* is pompous, rich, abundantly ornamental, has movement of the masses and makes particular use of various forms of arches and arched vaults. The Byzantine cupola is supported by four or eight pillars, on four if the plan is square, on eight, if it is hectagonal. The pillars are held together by arches. An essential element of Byzantine churches are the columns which form galleries and support the domes at the same time.

On the columns are the capitals, with acanthus leaves and animals, on which is almost always found a pulino decorated with reliefs. On the interior and external walls and on the ceilings is a very rich and shinning decoration of mosaics. This style was in vogue in Venice from the VI to the XII century.

THE ROMANESQUE STYLE. — It is the style which was prevalent at the beginning of the Middle Ages in the West and which was adopted by people of Roman Catholic religion. In Venice its presence is subordinate to the Byzantine style of the XI and XII centuries. It can be easily recognized because of the thick walls with tiny windows which make up the construction of the church. In the interior is a double line of pillars or columns, united by arches, which divides the church into three parts; the cross-vault is almost similar to the Byzantine.

THE GOTHIC STYLE. — It is so called because Italian artists of the Renaissance defined it in this way as it did not contain the ancient purity of style; for them « Gothic » was synonymous with barbarian. This style originated in northern France in the XII century; in Italy and in Venice it came from the XII to the XV century. Its main characteristics are: the ogival arch, bold and light vaults, the tendence everywhere towards an upward movement, large and tall windows divided in two or more parts by little columns, and finished above with ornaments pierced with geometrical figures.

RENAISSANCE STYLE. — It is so called because, in the first half of the fifteenth century, in contrast with Gothic forms, the great Italian architects got inspiration from pure Greek and Latin forms and adapted them to the necessities of

ARCHITECTURAL STYLES

The Byzantine Style   The Romanesque Style

The Gothic Style   Renaissance Style

their time. The main features of this style are: the plan of the church imitates the Roman basilica with the vaults and domes placed on a cylindrical construction with a lantern with small windows; the columns are formed by a shaft only, arches built upon one curve; the friezes and cornices and entablatures are complete, ornated vaults with paintings and reliefs, rectangular windows with rich cornices sustained by pillars and columns; rich and very beautiful ornaments assume sometime (especially in the late Renaissance) exaggerated proportions thus giving us a *Baroque style* in which prevails the curved over the straight line, thus giving us an original and bizarre decoration and a form of architcture in which each element is treated with the greatest liberty of conception.

FROM THE XI TO THE XIII CENTURY.

ARCHITECTURE: Byzantine architects, according to tradition, laid on three naves the Basilica of San Marco imitating, thus, the destroyed church of the Apostles. The plan is, in fact, in the form of a Greek cross. We shall see in the description of the basilica the various elements that make it up in different periods. In all probability these architects were assisted by local masters who felt the Lombard influence. The church of San Giacomo di Rialto is to be attributed to Venetian-Lombard architects; the church of San Fosca a Torcello and the Cathedral of Murano are also by the same artists.

PAINTING: We have at this period in Venice a kind of painting made up exclusively of mosaics, which derives from the close contacts with Byzantine art. Venetian mosaic cycles have a special characteristic all of their own which puts them out of reality; they can give high dramatic effects and peculiar contrasts of light and colour.
Of this painting we can see a live example in San Marco to the internal and external decoration of which, begun perhaps in the XII century, contributed mosaic workers from Constantinople who created trained groups who, with the passing of time, were capable of completing the immense mosaic work of the cathedral. The mosaic decoration of the Cathedral of Torcello was also of the same inspiration.

SCULPTURE: In sculpture also we note a radical adherence to Byzantine art. Numerous are, in fact, the sculptures which we find in San Marco and in other churches of the city due to unknown local artists who have been so adherent to Byzantyne inspiration to be even exchanged for masters from the East. But soon enough will be felt the influence of Lombard sculpture with Benedetto Antelami whose followers in Venice itself give a sample of their worth in the decoration of the arches above the biggest door of San Marco. Not indifferent to the refined Byzantine taste, they succeed in giving their sculptures a new spirit which makes them effective and synthetic in their livest representations.

THE FOURTEENTH CENTURY

ARCHITECTURE: In contrast with central Italy, where the Gothic style in architecture has been accepted with effects not

Church of Sts. Simeone and Giuda.

wholly respectful of the schemes from the other side of the Alps but tending instead towards decorative rather than constructive requisites, in Venice it becomes a complement on account of the persistence of Romanesque forms. We have an example in Santa Maria dei Frari which is attributed to Nicola Pisano according to a mistaken tradition. The very beautiful construction in three naves reaches a particular spaciousness in the harmony between the Romanesque and Gothic styles. In civil architecture Venice leads until flowery Gothic with the traditional decorative Byzantine form. Let us notice the Ca' d'Oro the construction of which will become the classical type of Venetian civil architecture. With Lombard artists work also Architects Giovanni and Bartolomeo Bon, the same people who rebuilt the Palazzo Ducale.

PAINTING: Venetian painting at this moment is personified by Paolo Veneziano who remains faithful to Byzantine-Gothic tradition. He loves abundant golden decorations and chromatic Byzantine values. In the same position we find Lorenzo Veneziano who, unlike the first one, can put into his figures a greater spirituality. Another artist of class of this period is the Paduan Guariento who can combine Byzantine stylistic motifs with those of Giotto and the Gothic style. He is the author of a complicated fresco in the Ducale Palace which represents « Paradise ».

SCULPTURE: Gothic sculpture assumes in Italy balanced, solid, and clear forms and, like those of the other side of the Alps, it is an integral part of architecture. In Venice this style is represented with wonderful adherence by Iacobello and Pier Paolo Dalle Masegne. They execute the statues of Iconostasi in Saint Mark with robustness of relief, in which Tuscan linear style is not absent.

THE FIFTEENTH CENTURY

ARCHITECTURE: Renaissance style did not have immediate success in Venice on account of the prevalence of flowery Gothic which had already created masterpieces in civil architecture. One can say that the new style made its appearance towards the end of the fifteenth century with the interest of artists from other parts of Italy. Thus we see Antonio Rizzo giving proof or his genius with the erection of the Foscari Arch in the Ducale Palace in which the new forms are admirably combined with elements of the flowery Gothic. In the very curious Church of Santa Maria dei Miracoli Pietro Lombardi and his sons Tullio and Antonio realize the most beautiful Renaissance temple in Venice. Another architect of value is the Bergamasque Mauro Coducci to whom are attributed many civil palaces, he puts at the side of the imaginative and free local architecture, sobriety of lines, proportion and clarity of rythm.

PAINTING: In Venice various artistic personalities belong to two families of painters: the Bellini and Vivarini families. These artists have been influenced by Mantegna. Iacopo Bellini has a sense of colour which he can graduate in a constructive form and gives to his works a thoughtful humanity. We note with him the influence of Florentine painters who are present in Venice; Antonio Vivarini di Murano can give his figures a particular psychological outlook.

Ducal Palace: the Tetrarchs.

Worthy of the same consideration is his brother Bartolomeo whose art derives from Mantegna, his sign is incisive, his colour assumes a singular brilliance.

Another very good painter was Carlo Crivelli born in the Paduan School and influenced by the Flemish. He is gifted with a particular sensitivity, delicacy of lines and colouristic luminosity. A follower of his father is Gentile Bellini, also dependent on Mantegna's art from whom he gets the sense of relief, and of monumentality. Deriving his art from Antonello da Messina, Giovanni Bellini is outstanding in the School of his father Iacopo; Bellini at first stays within the schemes of Mantegna and Donatello and understands the spirit of Renaissance painting according to the teachings of Piero della Francesca. Once in contact with Antonello da Messina his art acquires a true and personal compositive monumentality. On account of the colour every single figure of his expresses an apparent plasticity. We thus arrive to the great Vittore Carpaccio who is formed after Bellini. Carpaccio has the special gift of colour with suggestive effects and accents of vivacious dramatic aspect. We also note in this period various Venetian painters who are the followers of Bellini and Antonello such as Marco Basaiti, Alvise Vivarini, Cima da Conegliano, Vincenzo Catena and Bartolomeo Montagna da Vicenza. The latter is the most gifted of all on account of his austere composition and of his colour, thus beingable to create effects of plastic relief.

SCULPTURE: Gothic taste lasts until the middle of the fifteenth century. Lombard sculptors dictate laws with Matteo de' Raverti, although Florentine artistic personalities such as Lamberti, Giovanni di Martino da Fiesole and Nanni di Bartolo. A great sculptor, Bartolomeo Bon, with an ample sense of relief, makes the four « Virtues » on the door of the Carta of the Ducal Palace; his art betrays the influence of Dalle Masegne. After him we find Pietro Lombardi whose major work is the funeral monument to Doge Pietro Mocenigo in the Church of San Giovanni and Paul, his art aspires to formulas of classical plasticity, but in reality it is still faithful to effects of the past; Antonio Rizzo from Verona obtains effects of plasticity by coming very close to Tuscan art, he is the author of the project of the monument to Doge Tron ai Frari and is successful in creating a real masterpiece of plastic art in the two statues of Adam an Eve in the Foscari Arch in the Ducal Palace.

THE SIXTEENTH CENTURY

ARCHITECTURE: The solid sixteenth century architecture finds in Venice artists of high quality. First among all is the Florentine Iacopo Tatti called Sansovino whose constructions tend towards picturesque and chiaroscural effects in a sensible search for monumentality. By him we have the San Marco Bookshop, the Old Procuratie, the School of Misericordia, the Zecca, the Cornex Palace and the little loggia beneath the bell tower. One of his followers, Antonio da Ponte, is the architect of the Rialto and Sigh Bridges. But the real innovators in architecture in Venice and its region are Giovan Maria Falconetto, Michele Sanmicheli and Andrea Palladio; the former introduces in the laguna the classical Roman spirit, the latter obtains pictorial effects in the Grimani Palace, and the third brings an exceptional spatial-pictorial vision in the Church of S. Giorgio Maggiore and in the Redentore alle Giudecche.

Ducal Palace: the Judgement of Solomon.

To these great ones follows Vincenzo Scamozzi whose art
is in part imitative of Palladio and Sansovino. By him is
the entrance hall of the Bookshop, the New Procuratie,
and the Contarini-Scrigni Palace.

PAINTING: We must admit that colour has always found its leader in Venice. In this century, however, painters have adopted the light-shade principle which produces a kind of painting in which the line is conditioned to the mass and the relief is obtained by means of the graduation of shade and light. Of this kind of painting are a true and live expression Giorgio Barbarelli called Giorgione, Vecellio Tiziano; Iacopo Robusti called Tintoretto and Paolo Cagliari called Veronese. The School of these great ones attracts artists such Palma the Elder, Giovanni Antonio da Pordenone, Paris Bordone, Bonifacio de' Pilati, Andrea Meldolla called Schiavone and at last Lorenzo Lotto: a very original artist who at a certain moment succeeds in differentiating himself from the leaders of the school and in assuming a personality all of his own. Finally we note Sebastiano Luciani called Piombo.

SCULPTURE: Sculpture assumes in Venice a characteristic which is different from that of Donatello. At this period Venetian art prefers a quiet development of surfaces, thus obtaining effects of poetic reality while keeping its classical elements. In this atmosphere we find Tullio Lombardo together with his father Pietro and his brother Antonio. They are the authors of the decoration of S. Maria dei Miracoli. Venetian sculpture assumes a clear concreteness with the Florentine Iacopo Sansovino who brings in the works of art harmony and balance. From him get inspiration Danese Cattaneo, Tiziano Minio, and Andrea Vittoria.

THE SEVENTEENTH CENTURY

ARCHITECTURE: We have in Venice also what has taken place throughout Italy: namely, the advent of Baroque style defined as « a style of movement » in contrast with the Renaissance which has a limited vision of space: geometrically conceived and contained inside formal categories. The Baroque, instead, has no limitations whatsoever, it not only exalts a dynamic architecture thus obtaining curious pictorial effects, but also comes so close to the environment as to become an integral part of it. This tendency to movement and pictoricism manifests itself in Venice with Baldassare Longhena, a Venetian, grown up at the School of Scamozzi and influenced to a very great extent by the Florentine Sansovino.

PAINTING: At the beginning of the century Venetian painting contains still elements of sixteenth century artists. Painters such as Damiano Mazza, Andrea Vicentino, Palma the Younger, Aliense, Santi Peranda and Alexander Varotari called Padovanino move still in the orbit of Tiziano and Tintoretto. However a new current starts operating in the laguna itself through painters such as Bernardo Strozzi, Domenico Feti and Giovanni Lisa. These arrived in Venice at this period. The first, whose formation was Tuscan- mannerist, has felt the influence of Rubens and has for this reason a technique which puts in relief an exuberant colouristic sensibility; the second has thought how it is possible to combine past experiences with new ones and reach an original spontaneity; the third, a native of Oldenburg and influenced by Rubens, in his Venetian activity manifests a new taste, possesses a strong stroke in painting which creates new colouristic effects.

SCULPTURE: Venetian sculpture at this epoch is almost non-existant. Local artists depend still on the art of Sansovino and Vittoria. A new wave of inventive capacity is, however, brought to Florence from the outside. Among these are to remembered the Genovese Filippo Parodi, the Bolognese Giuseppe Mazza, the Flemish sculptor Giusto Le Court and Bernardo Falcone from Lugano.

THE EIGHTEENTH CENTURY

ARCHITECTURE: There is very little to say concerning architecture in Venice in the eighteenth century. We note, however, a strong reaction against Baroque tastes by enlarging and systematizing architectural structures of decorative exagerations. One of the major exponents of the above tendency is Giorgio Massari who, imitating Scamozzi, directly through Palladio, gives to Venice the Grassi-Stucky Palace and the Church of the Jesuits.

PAINTING: Venetian painting has an exceptional character in the eighteenth century. Through painting the Serenissima is once again the leader in Italy and in Europe by offering an artistic panorama which is ample and complex in the seriousness of its contents, colouristic richness, decorative sensibility and a more ample and sentimental vision. We list the greatest names in eighteenth century artists: Sebastiano Ricci, Giambattista Piazzetta, Giambattista Tiepolo, and his son Gian Domenico (who also were great engravers), Giambattista Pittoni, Rosalba Carriera, Nicola Grassi, Pietro and Alessandro Longhi, Giannantonio Pellegrini, Jacopo Amigoni, Marco Ricci, Giuseppe Zais, Francesco Zuccarelli. Also to be remembered are the famous « vedutisti » Antonio Canal called Canaletto, Luca Carlevaris, Bernardo Bellotto and the very great Francesco Guardi.

:SCULPTURE: A certain adherence to the great local painters, but without the height of their pictorial genius, characterizes the work of those sculptors who are successful in giving a demonstration of a superlative technical ability. Among the best ones are to be noted Giovanni Maria Morlaiter who in his scultures shows a light and vivacious touch as well as a research of atmospheric effects which gives to his images a persuasive spiritual sensibility. The activity of this artist has been very wide, he was helped by his son Gregory. Another artist of merit on account of his refinement and balance in his sculpture is Giovanni Marchiori the author of the « Sibyls » in the Scalzi chorus.

THE NINENTEENTH CENTURY

ARCHITECTURE: As far as this branch of art is concerned, in the midst of the neo-classical period, Venice is not influenced by the reelaboration of styles taking place in other parts of Italy. She maintains her traditional aspect without the slightest deviation.

PAINTING: Local pictorial art is similar to that of other cities in the peninsula; namely, it is permeated with the anti-classicist concept of form for chromatic and atmospheric values. Thus we have Giacomo Favretto who paints scenes of Venetian life a certain influence from eighteenth century schemes as well as from the art of Pietro Longhi. We also note Guglielmo Ciardi and Pietro Fragiacomo who go back to the traditional « vedutistica » Venetian tradition.

SCULPTURE: Venetian sculptors adhere to the neo-classicism of Antonio Canova; the only one who is opposed to it on account of technical and pictorial realism is Luigi Bozzo with a veiled aspiration to Romanticism.

THE CLOSE LOOK AT VENICE

We have so far given a general look at the history of the Serenissima; which has revealed to us her maritime and commercial power. We have also briefly realized the magnificence of
the incomparable city in the field of art; now it is necessary
to know Venice more intimately.

LIFE IN THE OPEN AIR.
On account of the urbanistic formation of the city, Venetians
are inclined to love light, air and sunshine; three elements
which are lacking, however, on account of the particular condition of their homes, especially in the popular quarters, which
face the calli, the rii, the rii-terra (that is to say those rii which
have become roads) which are as abundant as the poles that
support them. These houses have very steep staircases and very
small windows; those living at the last floor can enjoy a wooden
open gallery.
Windows and open galleries assume a peculiar appearance with
the hanging of the clothes, flower pots, and bird cages hanging
at the sides. Inside the house it is dark, thus the people go
out to the calli, the fields and little squares which become, especially during the summer, real living rooms. Here life goes on
in full swing because also of the many characteristic shops where
one can buy anything. It is this a daily life not very dissimilar
to that of the industrious and good Venetians of the good old
days. Of this cosmopolitan life the great Carlo Goldoni gives us
a very interesting picture in his plays.

OCCUPATIONS.
How do modern Venetians make a living? We know that the
city lacks real industries, but possesses workers of a traditional
experience (about one thousand years old) and which is also
reflected in the denominations of the various calli. It would
take too long to give the history of the various forms of occupations. Suffice to say that they all have a real artistic sense
both ancient and modern; we shall only mention the most important ones. First of all the glass industry the centre of which
is in the island of Murano since the year 1297. Everybody knows
the various forms and the little and large masterpieces which
the masters of this difficult art can produce; their works are
famous throughout the world. The second occupation is lace
work which has its base at the Island of Burano. Since ancient
times gentle hands, patiently,created real jewels for their designs and workmanship. We only have to realize that this essen-
tially feminine art reached so much importance that famous
artists put their great art to its service. Venetians were also
worthy workers — and they are to this day — as bronze workers,
goldsmiths, book binders, engravers, and very expert furniture
makers.

TRADITIONAL HOLIDAYS.
Many were the public holidays of the Queen of the Adriatic and
all had reference to historical events. Here we shall only mention
the most important ones of the past and the few ones which
take place in our days. In the past very solemn indeed was the
« Sensa » that is the Ascention during which on the little square
was held the « Fair », a real review of all products while the
Doge, aboard the Bucintoro and accompanied by ducal ships and
pontoons, went ahead with the ceremony of the « Wedding of the
Sea ». This celebration originated from the enlightened political and military action of Doge Pietro Orseolo II, who, in the
day of Ascension in the year 999 (May 18), defeated the Slavs.
This victory gave political and commercial power to the Republic.

Flight of pigeons in piazza San Marco.

To commemorate this event was instituted the ceremony of « The Wedding » of the sea. In a pompous uniform the Doge used to arrive at the harbour of the Lido. The Patriarch of Venice used to bless the symbolic nuptial ring, then, after pouring holy water into the sea, the Head of the State would throw the ring into the body of water saying: Oh sea! we marry you to show our real and eternal domain ».
Another holiday, no longer celebrated, was « Feast of the Mal rie » which started from a legendary rape by pirates of a few

girls who were about to get married. They were taken to a harbour near Caorle, but the Venetians went to their help and destroyed the pirates and brought back the young ladies. To commemorate this fact the 31 of January of each year, in the day of the translation of the body of Saint Mark, with great pomp, the presence of the Doge, and all authorities and a great number of people, twelve girls used to go to mass in Santa Maria Formosa. In this feast, which was soon abolished, the Venetian people had the opportunity of enjoying themselves during Jeudi Gras. This holiday also was due to a battle for religious reasons and which saw the destruction of Aquileia. Very famous was the « Venetian Carnival » during the period of political decadence of the Republic. We can say that all Europe was inspired from the gay and free life of the Serenissima especially noticeable during the period of Carnival.

Among the feasts that are still celebrated, we must remember that of the Presentation of the Virgin which takes place in Santa Maria della Salute. The church was built in 1631 to thank the Vergin for liberating the city from the terrible pestilence. For the celebration two bridges of boats are built across the Grand Canal. These bridges join the sections of S. Moisè and Santa Maria Zobenigo with the opposite banks, thus allowing the Patriarch and the Faithfuls in the procession to pay homage to the Byzantine Madonna surrounded with a myriad of candles as a symbol of gratitude and of the religious sentiment of the Venetian people. Another holiday is that of the « Redeemer » which takes place at night opposite the homonymous church of the Canal of Giudecca. In this occasion also we can see lighted barges wit flowers, artificial fires, abundant suppers before the people who enjoy the show from the opposite flanks. This celebration takes place in the night of the Saturday and the third Sunday in July. Another night holiday is the « Serenade »: it is a large, lighted boat decorated with rich ornaments on which take their place the orchestra, the chorus, and the singers. The parade proceeds numerous gondolas and other kinds of embarkations.

From the foundations of houses and places the population follows the parade listening to songs, recitals, music of ancient and modern opera. The first Sunday in Septembre marks the date of the great Regata which takes place on the Grand Canal. To this celebration participate the best gondoliers from the several quarters and islands of the city, they prove themselves in a very passionate race. They are preceded by a rich group of embarkations elegantly adorned. The Regata also has ancien origins, we know of its existence since the year 1300. The manifestations took place quite often as it was the way of welcoming famous guests.

VENETIAN COOKING.

We suggest that those who are guests in Venice, even if for one day only, will not offend waiters by asking for dishes and specialties from other regions of Italy, but will instead taste the excellent Venetian cooking. The main base of it being Adriatic fish treated by cooks in such special way that other Italian cities do not know. Ask for « mixed » rice (which contains shrimps), tasty « granseola » and « canestrelli in umido », the « folpeto » in oil or lemon, the delicious « bisato », the « dried cod-fish a la Vicentina ». For those who are allergic to fish we suggest « pasta and fasioi », « risi and bisi », « risi cola luganiga » diver and tripe in the Venetian style.

Two views of Piazzale Roma.

A VISIT TO THE CITY

Venice is of such unique and incomparable beauty that he who visit it for the first time is dazzled. A city which rises from the waters and which seems suspended between the sea and the sky is not something one can conceive unless one sees it with one's own eyes. The excitement of the visitor, foreigner or not, is such that as soon as he puts his feet on the vaporetto he is directed towards the heart of the city and arrives there through its main artery, through that marvelous street of water which is the Grand Canal. He is struck by the fantastic series of houses and palaces, looks at the left and at the right rapidly on account of the speed of the vaporetto without even being able to relize the suggestive and exciting beauty surrounding him. He is in a hurry to get there where has had its origin the long thread of the political and artistic history of the city, going through the centuries along rii and calli, canals and sestieri, creating a part of paradise in that great textile which is the Italian land.

Well, we want to greet the visitor as soon as he docks at Sain Mark and we want to accompany him to an external visit of the buildings which from the Ferry of Calle Vallaresso leads to the Piazzetta, to the Bank of Schiavoni and then to Saint Mark's Square, leaving out the Basilica of Saint Mark and the Ducal Palace of which we shall give an external and internal description at the end of our promenade into the heart of Venice.

From the pontile di San Marco at the piazzetta San Marco.

As soon as we have arrived at the landing-stage of Saint Mark, we are opposite a little palace of Lombard style of the XV century. In the past this palace was the residence of Magistrate della Farina, in 1750 the Academy of painters and sculptors of which was the president in 1756 G. B. Tiepoli, who remained as such until 1807. At present it is the headquarters of the Port Authorities. In the interior is a hall with a ceiling frescoed by Iacopo Guarana (1773) with the « Triuph of Art ». Continuing along we see the Gardens of the Royal Palace in the area of which rose in the past a long building used for the preservation of wheat. At the end of the royal gardens let us note the beautiful palace of Zecca, the

Partial view of the Grand Canal; to the left:
the Church of Santa Maria della Salute.

work of Sansovino (1535). The arcade studded with
rustic bosses, the first floor of Doric order and the second of Ionic give on the whole a sensation of force
and severity which is most fitting for the use made of
the Zecca Palace by the Republic. As a matter of fact
here were minted the famous golden Venetian sequins

31

which rivalled with the « golden florins » of Florence. The two systems were used throughout Europe and even in the Orient. In 1870 the Zecca was abolished and the palace contains since 1905 the reading hall of the Marciana National Library. Near the Zecca Palace is the most beautiful building of Renaissance style which Venice possesses, it is by the Florentine architect Iacopo Tatti called Sansovino. From its author it is called the *Sansoviniana Library* because it was destined to contain the precious ancient codes left as a gift to the Republic since 1468 by Cardinal Bessarione. The Library has a Doric arcade at the ground, an upper Ionic floor in the shape of a colonnade, a beautiful frieze, and the whole is crowned by a balustrade of classical inspiration with angular obelisks and statues of mythological divinities. Sansovino died at the age of 94 without completing the work which was finished between 1583 and 1588 by Vincenzo Scamozzi from Vicenza. The very beautiful building which Palladio defined « the riches and most ornated building since ancient times » is located along the Piazzetta (little square).

Piazzetta San Marco

We have thus arrived at the Piazzetta which can be defined the hall of the imposing Saint Mark's square. We admire the urbanistic whole of the Piazzetta: on one side the Library, on the other the flank of the Ducal Palace, in the background the Basilica of San Marco and the Clock Tower. With these monuments we shall concern ourselves in a while, after seeing the largest square in Venice. Let us stay in the Piazzetta and admire the Basin of San Marco, ample and splendid, which allows us to see the Island of S. Giorgio Maggiore with the beautiful church by Palladio: at the borders of the Piazzetta rises the column of San Todaro (San Teodoro) which is coupled with the other on which rests the Lion of San Marco.

The two granite columns were brought here from the Orient in the XII century. They were three columns at that time but one fell in the water in the landing operations and it has been impossibile to find it despite the intensive search. At any event the ones that we see were erected in 1772 by Niccolò Barattieri who was the builder of the first wooden bridge in Rialto. For

Piazzetta San Marco.

this work he was recompensed by being allowed to keep between the columns a bench for the hazardous game called « baratto » at that time. Baratto means barter. It seems that this game was the reason that Niccolò was given the last name of Barattieri. At this same spot was erected the set-up for capital executions.

Over the column that faces the Library of Sansovino we see the marble statue of San Teodoro, a Greek saint who was the first protector of the Venetians. A peculiarity of this statue is the fact that it is not made up of one block only; in fact its head is of Parian marble and, according to the experts, it is a very successful portrait of Mitridate the King of the Ponto (sea); the torso instead certainly originates from Rome at the time of Emperor Adrian, while the dragon on which rests the statue belongs to Lombard artists of the first half of the XV century. The capitol is of Venetian-Byzantine style. San Teodoro holds a shield at his right which means, according to an old author, that the Venetians have always aimed at defending themselves rather than offending. At the present the base as well as the statue have been substituted with copiose and the originals are found in the Ducal Palace.

The other column, on a Venetian-Byzantine capitol, has the bronze statue of the Lion of Saint Mark which at one time was gilded. It is not known where the Venetians have found this sculpture which art experts attribute to Etruscan or to Persian or Chinese art; at any event much-discussed sculpture attracted the French when in 1797 they entered Venice .They transported it to Paris but was brought back in 1815 after being restored and in part reshaped on account of serious damages.

PONTE DEI SOSPIRI - RIVA DEGLI SCHIAVONI

Past the Ducal Palace we come across the Bridge called of the Paglia (Straw) because it was here that the straw destined to the prisoners was unloaded. The bridge passes over the Rio di Palazzo where one can admire the very famous Bridge of Sighs, a Baroque construction which unites the Ducal Palace with that of the Prison - it is so called on account of the sighs of the prisoners passing from here to appear before the inquisitors. The bridge has been built by Antonio Contini about 1600 by will of Doge Marino Grimani. Passed the Bridge of Paglia we find the ex-Palace of the Prisons with one

Bridge of Sighs.

floor of classical style with a robust open arcade. It was built before 1589 and completed in 1614 by Architects Antonio da Ponte, G.A. Rusconi and Tommaso Continuo.

From here begins the Schiavoni Bank which is so called because here landed with their ships the Dalmatians from Schiavonia. In ancient times the bank was as wide as the Bridge of Paglia, in 1324 it was paved with stone and 1780 the Senate decreed that the above-named bridge be widenend to reach that of the Ca di Dio. Today the bank is five hundred meters long and constitutes one of the most beautiful walks in Venice. On the bank is the Dandolo Palace with the beautiful facade built in the XV century. It became later the property of the Gritti, Bernardo and Mocenigo families, until it was purchased by a certain Danieli who restored it and made of it one the most luxurious and hospitable hotels in Venice. A little further, past the bridge, is the Church of S. Maria della Pietà of 1760 of eighteenth century style by Architect Giorgio Massari. In its interior is a frescoed ceiling by G.B. Tiepolo which represents the Cardinal Virtues - above the entrance to the choir is a cloth by Alessandro Bonvicino called Moretto da Brescia, which « Jesus in Simone's House » (1544) originating from the Convent of S. Fermo at Monselice. Past the Bank of Schiavoni the walk continues along the Bank of Ca' di Dio, San Biagio and the Seven Martyrs which leads to the public gardens where has its headquarters the International Exposition of Modern Art.

PIAZZA SAN MARCO

At this point it is necessary to go back, going along the Piazzetta and turn one's back to the Marciana Basilica in order to enjoy the view of Saint Mark's Square, the great open hall of the Venetians which is sumptuous and unique in the world. It has known the splendours of life of all times, celebrations, joys, sorrows of many generations to which have contributed humble and wealthy citizens olike. How did this immense square begin to taken shape? The answer is given to us by a Venetian who knew everything about his city: Giuseppe Tassini. In his book entitled « Venetian Curiosities » he expresses himself in this way: « Rustic was in ancient times the Square of Saint Mark. It was called « Morso », perhapes on account of its unusual hard and resistant soil, and « Brolo » (orchard) because it was full of grass and surrounded with trees. In the middle flew a canal called « Batario » on the banks of

Riva degli Schiavoni.

which rose, one opposite the other, the two little churches of San Teodaro and San Gemignano, erected, as we well know, by Narsete who had defeated the Gori and with the help of Venetian boats ».

At that time were being built the Basilica of San Marco and the Ducal Palace, thus, all the green space in front of the constructions, in the period of the reign of Doge Sebastian Ziani (1172-78), was arranged with the burial of the Batario reaching thus its actual surface. At the sides were built beautiful houses with arcades, in some of which lived the Procurators of Saint Mark who gave these buildings the name of Procuratie.

In 1264 the square was paved with bricks arranged in the shape of a fish skeleton and it remained in this way until 1723 when, after a design of Andrea Tirali, it was paved with trachyte and white bands.

Actually the square, which is in the shape of a trapeze, is 175½ meters long, 82 meters wide in front of the facade of the Basilica and 57 meters on the opposite side.

Torre dell'Orologio

Looking at the right the first thing that strikes us is the Clock Tower built by Mauro Coducci between 1496 and 1499. The lateral wings were added in 1500-1506 apparently after a project by Pietro Lombardi; they were later raised by Giorgio Massari (1755). The tower is crowned by a terrace on which is the Bell which, hit by two virile figures called «Mori», has been indicating time for over four and one half centuries. The Moors were cast in bronze by Ambrogio da le Anchore in 1497. Under the crowning of the tower we note the coat-of-arms of Venice; namely, the winged lion. Immediately under the coat-of-arms we see a small, semicircular terrace with a niche and two lateral doors. In the niche is the Madonna and Child in gilded copper, perhaps the work of Alessandro Leopardi, the sculptor and goldsmith born in the second half of the 1400 century and deceased in 1522-23.

During the day of the Ascension, and for the whole week of such celebration, the Magi Kings come out of their doors and low before the Virgin. The gentle tradition has lasted to our day and costitutes one of the most unique attractions for visitors who happen to be in Venice at this time. Under the semicircular terrace we see the large clock-face of the complex mechanical clock put there at the end of the fifteenth century by Giampaolo and Giancarlo Ranieri, father and son, from Parma. The clock indicates the passing of the seasons, the passing of the sun from one to another constellation, the hours and lunar phases; it was restored in 1757 by Bartolomeo Ferracina.

A nice view of the Clocktower.

Procuratie Vecchie - Ala Napoleonica - Procuratie Nuove

After the Tower of the Clock is the *Procuratie Vecchie* with two stories of loggias; they were built between the end of the 1400 and the middle of the 1500. The plan of the construction is apparently by Mauro Coducci who built the first floor of the building; to him suceeded after the fire of 1512 Bartolomeo Bon and Guglielmo Grigi who made almost all the work except for the very last part which was completed by Sansovino. The Procuratie Vecchie, so called in order to differentiate them from the new which were built later, have been created by following the pre-existing architectural motif; they constitute a harmonic whole which gives the square an usurpassed solemnity. The side in the back of the square where once existed the ancient church of San Gemignano, was demolished in 1807 by will of the Emperor of the French Napoleon I to make room for a grand ball room to which one has access from the Royal Palace.

Thus this is the very new Wing or Napoleonic Wing built in neo-classical architecture by Architect Giuseppe Soli, who repeats the two orders of the New Procuratie, crowned by an attic with statues of Roman emperors, mythological and allegorical figures. At the left side are the New Procuratie which were begun to be built by Vincenzo Scamozzi in 1584. He got inspiration from the neoclassical style of the Sansoviniana Library and carried ahead the construction to the tenth arch; it was later continued and completed by Baldassare Longhena in 1640. Here also resided the Procurators of San Marco, but when the Republic fell in 1797, the New Procuratie were at the Royal Palace.

At present they are the headquarters of important art and culture institutes such as the Archeological Museum and the Correr Museum.

Basilica and Campanile of St. Mark's.

Piazza
San Marco -
Above: to
the left, **the
Procuratie
Nuove
by Vincenzo
Scamozzi
(1584);** in the
background,
**Napoleonic
Wing
by Giuseppe
Soli (1807).**
Below:
**The Procuratie
Vecchie built
between 1400
and 1500,**
perhaps the
work of
Codussi.

Campanile

The sixth personality of the square is the massive bell-tower. It was the most ancient in Venice because it was erected on Roman foundations at the time of Doge Pietro Tribuno (889-912); built in many stages it was the work of Niccolò Barattieri and Bartolomeo Malfatto for the cell, Proto Bon and Giorgio Spaventa. This Campanile had stood for centuries storms and earthquakes; finally, tired of all this suffering and on account of the weak construction; it collapsed the 14 of July 1902 at 10:00 A.M. There were no human victims and little damage to the near-by monuments except for the burial of the Loggetta Sansoviniana which was broken to pieces but finally brought together piece by piece. The bell-tower was rebuilt « where it was and as it was » and inaugurated in 1912 the day of the Patron of Venice. All Venetians acclaimed the « parco de casa » (house boss) as they wittingly call it; it is in fact the house boss because high from the room of the bells one can enjoy the most complete view of the city and the lagoon. The bell-tower is 98 meters and 60 centimeters high.

On top of the cusp a gilded Angel turns with the direction of the wind. We can reach the bell room by means of an elevator.

With the collapse of the bell tower four bells out of five were broken and the Angel was ruined with the Loggetta; the whole was repaired by the very patient Venetian artist Emanuele Munaretti. The five bells have peculiar names and each had a particular function: the Marangona whose strokes used to call to work the joiners (Marangoni) giving the signal of the beginning and the end of the work to all Venetian workers, it indicated midnight and was silent during the holidays; then we have the Mona which gave the signal of noon; the Trottiera so called because at its sounding the Patricians went to the Senate riding a horse when the city was partially paved; the Pregadi because it announced the reunion of the Grand Council; the Renghiera or Maleficio, also called of Justice, because it rang for half an hour during capital executions.

Moreover on the bell tower on the side of the square, at certain height, was a cage inside which were exposed day and night all those guilty of crimes, a pillory which was abolished towards the middle of the XVI century. Connected with the bell tower was also the « flight of the Angel » in the last thursday of Carnival. A cord was placed between the bell room and the Loggia of the Ducal Place and an acrobat. protected by a cord, slided as far as the end where he found the Doge offering him a bouquet of flowers.

Emperors, kings, cardinals, ambassadors went up the bell-tower; but the most illustrious of all was Galileo Galilei who wanted to explain to the Signoria the usefulness of his telescope.

Loggetta

At the base of the bell tower is the wonderful *Loggetta* (of three arches) by Sansovino, of Renaissance style, with four beautiful statues in bronze made by the same. It was built between 1537 and 1549 in substitution of another of the XIII century, existing at first in the zone of S. Basso and transported here. In 1569 the Loggetta was the headquarters of the armed Guard of the Republic during the sessions of the Major Council. The very beautiful statues adorning it give us an example of the high plastic value reached by Sansovino in the period of his full maturity, they represent Apollo, Mercurio, Peace and Minerva. Each has a particular meaning referring to the activity of the Serenissima; Apollo personifies the power of the Republic. Mercurio the eloquence of his ambassadors and men of cultur, Peace is the concept to which the Venetians are sworn to and Minerva the height of genius in politics, war, in arts and knowledge.

The very beautiful gate in bronze is the work of Antonio Gai (1735), by him are also the putti at the extremities of the attic, while the allegorical bas-relief (of Venetian power) are attributed to Tiziano Minio and Danese Cattaneo. In front of the Basilica we note three Javelins in bronze on which in former times were raised the flags of the Republic. All three are real works of art made in 1505 by the sculptor and goldsmith Alessandro Leopardi, the one at the centre is particularly interesting because it shows in the shape of a medal, the energetic profile of Doge Leonardo Loredan.

Loggetta, by Sansovino (detail).

THE BASILICA OF SAINT MARK

Its history: — The Cathedral of Venice rises with the consolidation of the power of the Republic on the sea. In the year 828 arrived the spoils of the Evangelist Saint Mark subtracted from the profane Mussulmans of Alexandria, Egypt. Welcomed with solemn ceremonies the spoils were at first located in the Chapel of the « Palatium »; namely, the little church of San Teodoro, - But for Saint Mark now become the new and only Patron of the Serenissima, Doge Giustiniano Partecipazione left a large sum for the construction of a basilica worthy in every way of containing such precious relics. His desire was satisfied by his brother Giovanni Partecipazio who began the great construction beside the Ducal Palace bringing it to an end in 832 for the walling and in 883 for the decoration. In 976 an uprising of the people against the despotism of Doge Pietro Candiano IV occurred and fire was started in the Ducal Palace; the flames invested even the Basilica which was restored after a few years by Doge Pietro Orseolo, the Saint. After the year one thousand Doge Dominic Contarini judged the Basilica inadequate for the times, especially because in the cities of the terra firma were growing magnificent Romanesque basilicas. For this reason he had the church demolished and had it rebuilt it as we see it nowadays. The works begun in 1063, according to a few historians and later according others, were not completely finished during the Dogeship of Contarini. He had chosen the scheme of Byzantine churches in Greek plan with domes, interpreted however in a Romanesque sense. We still' do not know who the architect was.

The building was completed in 1073. The primitive temple of Contarini had an austere and empty appearance, but soon enough was begun its very beautiful decoration of mosaics, was enriched with precious marbles originating from Altino; from the Orient arrived various architectural elements and bas-reliefs; Byzantine, Gothic, Islamic and Renaissance styles adorned the magnificent temple.

Admirals and merchants brought from the conquered cities, or with those which traded with them, the most precious things they could find to beautify the great temple of the Republic; this temple which had become the symbol of its power. The golden basilica, in which everything is poetry and warmth, is a complex masterpiece of art which has been slowly created in time with the participation of famous artists and for merit of the very able Venitian administrators. We will become aware of these things in a visit in the interior and in the exterior.

THE WORKS OF ART:

THE FACADE. — Let us stay at a convenient distance on the square in order to admire with only one glance the very beautiful effect of the external architectural complex (which is 51,80 meters long). Please note the doors with the oblique system of arches towards the interior according to Romanesque style and which have their corresponding in the above arches, horizontally divided by the thin balustrade, with the alert horses. Higher up are the five domes which have an all-Oriental charm. Ibe whole obeys to a scenographic concept which completes the incomparable square. This concept will uniform the whole Venetian architecture no matter what the style for Alms ». Left of the altar is the entrance to the Aula will be.

Main façade of St. Mark's Basilica. ▶

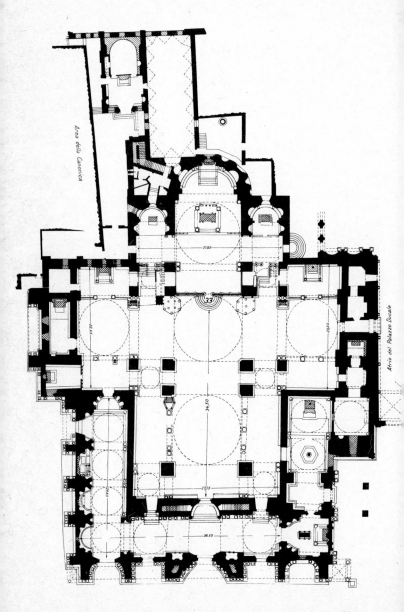

Area della Canonica

Atrio del Palazzo Ducale

Now, with the topographical map, following the internal and external numeration of the basilica, let us admire the works of art which we shall give brief hints by citing only the most important ones. Before beginning our numeration, however, let us note the right flank of the Basilica which faces the Ducal Palace. We are immediately struck by the curious sculptural group in porphyry of the four Tetrarchs who affectionately hug one another; the group is of Egyptian or Syrian origin and there are those who claim that they represent Emperors Diocletian, Massimian, Valerius and Costanzo. Not far away we note two square pillars brought here by Saint John from d'Acri in Syria. On the wall of the Basilica above, is a Byzantine Madonne before which are two lamps kept always lighted to commemorate the legend of the poor « Little Baker of Venice » who was sentenced for a crime he had not committed. At the corner of the square « Pietra del Bando » is a portion of a column of Syrian origin on which used to go the « banditore » (broadcaster) who was entrusted with the duty of reading to the people the law as approved by the government.

NOW LET US BEGIN THE EXTERNAL NUMBERING

1. - Portal with a rich Moorish decoration. Above ,in the mosaic is represented the fleeing of the Body of Saint Mark, a seventeenth century work by Pietro Vecchia.

2. - In the second portal, always by Pietro Vecchia, is the mosaic representing the arrival in Venice of Saint Mark.

3. - Central door: let us note ·the gracious bas-relief by Venetian-Roman artists. They have depicted the professions, the months of the year, virtues and other symbols. Above the door is a beautiful Romanesque sculpture of the XII century « An Angel appears to Saint Mark »; above, in the mosaic; « Universal Judgement made by Lattanzio Querena in 1836.

4. - In the fourth portal let us note the bronze door by Maestro Bertuccio in 1300. Above a mosaic by Sebastiano Ricci (1728) shows the Venetians rendering homage to the Body of Saint Mark.

5. - The fifth portal is called of Saint Alipio from the statue of this Saint which was at one time located in the upper kiosk. It is decorated with columns, capitals, bas-reliefs of pagan and Byzantine origin, taken from more ancient churches.

View of the main façade of St. Mark's Basilica.

Above is a mosaic which goes back to 1260-70 and which represents the « Transportation of Saint Mark's Body ». His mosaic is especially interesting because it shows us how the facade of the Basilica was at that time. *The upper floor of the facade*: he who wishes to see closely the works of the upper floor after the visit to

the interior of the Basilica will have access into the
terrace through appropriate galleries. We, to complete
the cycle of the facade, suggest the visitor to be at a
convenient distance on the square so that he can
include everything in his glance. Thus, under the
elegant marble thread of the terrace, between one arch

St. Mark's
Basilica:
Central door
with the
mosaic lunette
representing
the " Last
Judgement ".

and another of the lower floor, we note very beautiful Byzantine bas-reliefs of the XII century. They represent: (from left to right) Hercules and the Wild Oar, the Madonna, Saint George, Saint Demetrius, Archangel Gabriel and finally Hercules with the hind.

On the loggia, above the main door, stand in all their beauty the four gilded copper horses which Doge Henry Dandolo brought to Venice from Constantinople in 1204. They have been made in the IV century B.C. They were put in their actual position about 1250, in 1798 they attracted Napoleon's attention who took them to Paris, they were brought back to Venice in 1815 and twice they were transported in safe places because of the first and second world wars. Behind the horses we see four octagonal columns with beautiful capitals that go back to the XI century and the large windows of the major arcade, while in the minor ones at the two sides, above, we note beautiful mosaics

Piazzetta dei Leoncini.

The four gilded horses of St. Mark's Basilica.

by Maffeo da Verona. They represent: (from left to right) Deposition, Descent from the Limbo, Resurrection and Ascension. Worthy of the same consideration as the complex of the upper floor is the great statues that decorate the upper floor and which can be defined one of the most famous aggregates of Gothic Italian sculpture. It is believed to have been started by the Dalle Masegne in 1385, and after the fire of 1419, restored, continued and remade by Florentine and Lombard artists.

LEFT FLANK OF THE BASILICA, LITTLE SQUARE OF THE LEONCINI, AND DOOR OF THE FLOWERS. — Let us now take a look at the left flank where we find the Piazzetta dei Leoncini, so called on account of two lions in marble made by Giovanni Bonazza in 1722. Before the Door of Flowers let us not the three big arches and the beautiful Gothic sculptures of the crowning. In the middle of the first big arch is the symbolic figuration of the Apostles (12 lambs), right after it is « Alessandro Magno brought to Heaven » of the X century. It is situated between the first and the second arch. We arrive at the door of the Flowers which has preserved nothing of the ancient construction and goes back very easily to around 1200 when this part was retouched. Let us note the arch of Arab-Moorish style with a rich decoration of branches and flowers (from here the name of the door), in the lunette is a bas-relief representing the « Christmas Scene ». After the fourth arch, in the protrution, let us admire the five bas-reliefs, Byzantine works of the XII and XIII century, the most notable is that of « Christ Blessing and the Four Evangelists».

Continuing along, under a big arcade, is the Tomb of Daniel Manin, the work of Luigi Borro. Manin died in Paris in 1857 and his spoil were brought back to Venice in 1868. On the little square is the Baroque facade of the suppressed church of San Basso, perhaps the work of Giuseppe Benoni made about 1670.

In the middle is a marble fountain in the shape of a well, in the back is the Patriarchal Palace with a neo-classical facade by Lorenzo Santi (1837-50).

HALL OF THE BASILICA.

HALL OF THE BASILICA. — To have a complete vision of the hall and of its beauty it is necessary to pass through the central door of the facade.

The hall, a precious gallery which is all a collection of mosaic, with almost sharp-angled arcades which divide it into spans closed by five little hemispheric domes, while the central one before the door of which we have entered, is open. The hall, which is 62 meters long, 6 wide and 7,35 high, has preserved its primitive apearance and has seven hundred years of life; it has a marble floor with mosaics which assumes very beautiful effects of luminosity when « the high water » penetrates into it on account of its inferior level if compared with that of the church. The walls of the hall are decorated with columns of different origins and it seems that a few have been removed from the temple of Salomon in Jerusalem. By following the numbering of the plan of the large arcade we shall see the numerous mosaics which have episodes of the Old and New Testament. Almost all mosaics are the work of Venetian guilds who have expressed themselves with lively and effective Romanesque language, adopting a technique which reaches the highest expression for its colouristic effects and narrative synthesis.

Let us go to the back of the hall on the left hand side:

" Carrying the body of St. Mark ", mosaic of the lunette.

" The Venetians paying hommage to the body of St. Mark ",
mosaic of the lunette.

7. - We are before the Door of Flowers, in the back is the Door of Saint John. Above are the « Stories of Moses » which occupy the dome and the lunette, in the vanes are the figures of Salomon, David, Zachariah and Malachia. In the calotta above the Door of Saint John is a « Madonna and Child » between Saint John and Saint Mark ».

8. - Let us note in the calotta mosaic made from cartoons by Pietro Vecchia in the year 1600. They represent «Saint Apollinaire and Sigismond », and « Saint Francis with the stigmata ». In the dome is « Stories of Joseph » of the year 1200, in the vanes the « Evangelists » and, worthy of special attention, is « the beautiful Saint John ».

9. - Continuing along we have « the Stories of Joseph »; in an ancient sarcophagus, is the tomb of Doge Marino Morosino who died in 1953.

10. - In the calotta is a mosaic, « Judgement of Salomon » made by Giuseppe Bianchini from a cartoon by Salviati in 1583. The dome presents « Stories of Joseph « and in the vanes are four Hebrew prophets; the whole goes back to 1240, but have been restored in 1800. In the hall a Gothic-Pisan sculptor has worked on the tomb of Doge Bartolomeo Gradenigo who died in 1342.

11. - In the lunette of the Door of Saint Peter is a Byzantine mosaic depicting the same saint, while in the dome and in the lateral lunettes are « Episodes of Abraham's life » of Byzantine-Romanesque style. fluence of the School of Ravenna. Let us note the knockers of the entrance portal of the church with figures of Saints made in the period 1112-38.

12. - In the vault is a mosaic of the year 1200 called « Drunkeness and Death of Noah, the construction of the Tower of Babel and Dispersion of the people ». In the wall is the sepulchre of Felicita Michiel the wife of Doge Vitale Falier who died in 1101.

13. - In the niches above is a « Madonna and Saints », below the « Apostles ». Built in 1100 they feel the in-

St. Mark's Basilica: partial view of the interior.

Mosaics of St. Mark's: Christ enthroned.

The mosaic of the calotta is the work of Valerio
and Francesco Zuccato who composed it in 1945 after
a design by Titian and represents « Saint Mark in
Ecstasy ». By the same mosaic artists are also the
decorations of the vault with cartoons supplied by
Pordenone in 1549; they represent; Resurrection of
Lazarus, Crucifixtion, Deposition, Death of the Madonna ». In the vanes are figures of Evangelists and

Mosaics of St. Mark's: Jesus arrives in Jerusalem (détail).

Prophets. Let us note in the floor a red marble band which reminds us of the spot where the 23 of July 1777 Emperor Frederic Barbarossa knelt before Pope Alexander III.

14. - In the vault of the arcade are fifteen Stories of Noah » and of the « Universal Flood ». In the exterior side of the arcade, in a niche, is the tomb of Doge Falier who died in 1096.

15. - Here opens the Door of Saint Clement which is interesting for its bronze knockers divided into 28 rectangular portions, each of which carrying the figure of a saint with underneath a Greek silver description, of Byzantine execution and originating from Constantinople. In the lunette is another mosaic by Valerio Zuccato « Saint Clement » made in 1532. The dome (in

the fist, second and third zone) is decorated with mosaics, (1230) which refer to numerous episodes of the Bible: it begins with the « Creation of the Sky and the Earth » and ends with the « Story of Cain and Abel ».

16. - We are at the central door of entrance to the Basilica, at the left a little door covers the entrance to the galleries and to the Museum.

THE INTERIOR OF THE BASILICA. — Past the portal we have the suggestive and brilliant vision of the basilica divided into three naves of very great architectural simplicity. The plan is in the shape of a Greek cross on which are five large domes sustained by large pillars. The loggias recurring all around the church are supported by robust columns of precious marble with gilded capitols and are of Byzantine style. The mosaic floor of coloured marble and of rich design are of the XII century and has been rebuilt for the greatest part. It presents an uneven level because of the varied consolidation of the whole building which rests on embankment of piles.

The church, including the hall, is 76,50 meters in length, and 62,60 meters across the transept; the central dome is 43 meters high in the exterior and 28,15 meters in the interior. When the church was built, the Doge said to the unknown architect that it should be «the most beautiful one could possibly conceive». The result was not disappointing; there are splendid and luminous mosaics that cover altogether over four thousand square meters of space. This work with a gold background has lasted centuries; very capable Venetian guilds have contributed to it, together with the collaboration of great Venetian and Tuscan artists of the Renaissance. The whole decoration adheres to the concept of the exaltation of the Church of Christ. It is not easy to describe so many works of art, be they in sculpture, in architecture, or in mosaics. We shall limit ourselves to those works which may be seen by following the numbering of the plan. Whoever wants to enjoy more the vision of the mosaics can go up to the galleries.

Mosaics of St. Mark's: The Miracle of St. Mark (detail).

17. - Above the central door is a fourteenth century mosaic with « Christ Blessing between the Madonna and Saint Mark ». In the above-lying arch is the great mosaic of the « Apocalypse » made according to the visions of Saint John. It is the work of Pordenone and of the Zuccatos (1570-89). Behind this, against the central window, is the Big Arch of Paradise containing the powerfully conceived « Scenes of Universal Judgement » (centuries XVI and XVII). Many artists have contributed to the creation of this truly grand work; including among others, and Iacopo Tintoretto, Antonio Vassillacchi, Maffeo Verona, D. Tintoretto.

18. - DOME OF THE PENTECOST: It is very suggestive. At the cenre is the white pigeon which is the symbol of the Holy Spirit, whose divine blow, in the shape of tongues of fire, irradiates the seated Apostles. Between the small arched windows are depicted cathechized nations and in the four vanes are «Angels» of monumental impostation. These mosaics go back to the first half of 1100.

19. - LEFT LATERAL NAVE: Found here are the admirable mosaics depicting Jesus among four Prophets, (1200). Between the precious marble of the wall above is « Paradise and Triumph of the Trinity » by G. Pilotti, the « Martyrdom of Apostles Peter and Paul » by Palma Giovanni and Padovanino. In the right arch let us note « Crucified Saint Andrews » by Aliense; « Murder of Saint Thomas » by Tizianello; and in the one at the left by Padovino we admire « The miracles of Saint John ». This series of mosaics are of the year 1600.

20. - CAPITAL OF THE CRUCIFIX. A little chapel in hexagonal shape made up of six marble columns with Byzantine capitals. On the altar is painted a Crucifix which is thought to originate from Consantinople (1205) and, according to a sacred popular tradition, it is in a bloody condition because of a stab from a local citizen.

21. - The placement of Venetian mosaics on the great « Western Arch » can give the «Scenes of Passion» (1200) a truly moving and dramatic inspiration. The various episodes are so well-known that all can easily identify them in the five zones into which they are divided. A particular artistic interest is presented to us by the dramatic « Crucifixion ».

22. - In the vault and in the wall are very beautiful mosaics which have reference to episodes of the life of the Madonna and of the childhood of Jesus. Those in the vault go back to the years 1200 and 1300; those in the wall are of 1500 and have had the cooperation of artists such as Iacopo Tintoretto and Iacopo Palma the Younger.

23. - THE MASCOLI CHAPEL. It was founded in 1430 and assumed this name in 1618 when its ownership passed to an all male fraternity. The sculptures that we se there are attributed to the Bons; the very beautiful mosaics made between 1430 and 1450 refer to five episodes of the Life of the Virgin.

Michele Giambono is the author of the two episodes at the left, while at the right the « Visitation » and « Death of the Madonna » have been made on cartoons of Iacopo Bellini and Andrea Mantegna.

24. - CHAPEL OF SAINT ISIDORO. It was built by Doge Andrea Dandolo between 1354 and 1355 to contain the body of the Saint who is above the altar and whose tomb is sculptured in Gothic-Venetian style. On the walls and the vault are fourteenth century mosaics, vigorously concieved, which tell us the fifteen episodes of the life of the Saint.

25. - DOME OF SAINT JOHN. Here are found mosaics of 1200 of Venetian-Byzantine style representing episodes of the Saint's life, in which we note Romanesque influences. In the vanes are four saints, two of which are the work of Giambattista Piazzetta: «Saint Gregory and Saint Jerome».

26. - CHAPEL OF THE NICOPEIA MADONNA. Before entering the chapel let us note at the left, against the pillar, the « Altar of Saint Paul », a very beautiful work of sculpture of Renaissance style. The frontal with the bas-relief, « Conversion of Saint Paul », seems to have been the work of Pietro Lombardo.

In the Madonna Nicopei Chapel (victorious) who is much worshiped by the Venetians and considered by them their patron, is a beautiful Byzantine painting with Oriental enamels going back to the year one thousand. It was brought from Constantinople to Venice by Doge Enrico Dandolo in 1204. The altar is the work of Tommaso Contino (1617) and the sculptures which we see, « Madonna and Saints », go back to the XI and XII centuries and are of Venetian-Byzantine style.

Beneath the arches are decorative mosaics remade in 1600.

27. - In the great « Northern Arch » the mosaics represent: « The Wedding in Cana » and « Supper at Simone's House » made from cartoons by Iacopo Tintoretto; « Christ Healing the Leprous » by P. Veronese; and « Resurrection of the Son of the Window of Naim », by Giuseppe Salviati. In the small internal vault of the arch are four prophets.

28. - Here is the entrance to the Crypt of Saint Mark underlying the presbytery. Once we have gone down the little staircase we are in a place of cross vaulting sustained by Greek and Byzantine columns. The body of Saint Mark was put here in 1094. At one time the crypt was invaded by the waters as its level was under that of the Laguna. After much hard word it was restored and reopened to worship in 1889.

29. - CHAPEL OF SAINT PETER. An inconostasis with five statues of Saints attributed to the School of the Dalle Masegnes, precedes the Chapel. On the little altar a bas-relief represents the Saint, a fourteenth century work of the Venetian School. The mosaics which we see on the walls narrate episodes from the life of Saint Mark and Peter. They have been made in the second half of the XIII century. Through a door behind the altar of Saint Peter we can enter the *Sacresty,* while through another on the left side we can go into the *Little Church of Saint Theodor.* The beautiful *Sacresty* built in 1486, has a ceiling decorated with mosaics. In the vault the Christ at the centre is probably the work of Titian, the four Evangelists that surround him and a few figures of Apostles whom we see in the lunettes of the right wall reveal to us the art of Lorenzo Lotto, while in the calotte of the portal the « Eternal Father » is by Padovanino. At the sides of the door the « Two Saint Jeromes », made after a contest in 1563, are by Domenico Bianchini, called Rosso, and by the nephew Giannantonio. On three sides in the back let us note the very beautiful cupboards with tarsias depicting «Stories of Saint Mark », « Dead Natures » and « Landscapes ». They have been made by several artists, but the

Mosaics of St. Mark's: Jesus in the garden (detail).

whole composition seems inspired by one artist only whose style reminds us of the drawing ability of Vittore Carpaccio and to him critics attribute the cartoons for the execution of the valuable bread-cloths. The *Little Church of S. Theodore* also has become an aggregate of the Sacresty. It follows Renaissance architectural form and in the past it was the headquarter of the Tribune of the Inquisition. Above the altar are sculptures by Sansovino and in the wall Pietro Vecchia has given superlative proof of his art with the mosaic, « San Giovanni Begging for Alms ». Left of the altar is the entrance to the Aula Capitolare which possesses various paintings of value: let us note the « Adoration of the Shepherds » by G.C. Tiepolo and the portraits of the ecclesiastical chiefs executed by artists dependent on the schools of Gentile Bellini, Titian, B. Strozzi, P. Longhi. Let us admire the altar-piece by the latter of « Saint Lorenzo Giustinian and a little Cleric ».

30. - APSE. The passage leading to the apse leaves from the Chapel of Saint Peter. In the bowl of the apse is the « Blessing Christ » remade by a mosaic artist of 1500. Between windows we note the most ancient mosaics in the Basilica done in Byzantine style. The were not hurt by the fire of 1106 and represent the saints: Nicholas, Peter, Mark and Ermagora. The door which leads into the sacresty is the work of Sansovino.

31. - HIGH ALTAR AND DOME OF THE PRESBYTERY. The high altar is surmounted by a tribune which is supported by four precious columns of Oriental alabaster covered with basreliefs depicting episodes of the life of Christ and of Mary, a very beautiful work by Venetian sculptors of 1200. The statues above depict the Redeemer and the four Evangelists. Left of the ciborium are four bronze statues. « The Evangelists » are by Iacopo Sansovino; on the opposite side are four statues representing the « Doctors of the Church », the work of Girolamo Paliari of 1614. The table of the High Altar contains the Body of Saint Mark. Above the table of the altar is the famous and marvelous « Golden Altar-piece », a masterpiece in gold work by the Venetian Giampaolo Boninsegna (1345). Its measurements are 3,40 meters in width, and 1,40 in height. Originally it had been ordered from artists of Constantinople in 978, and was remade later in 1105 with gold and enamels originating from the Monastery of the Pantocrator at the time of the

fourth Crusade. It was Boninsegna who thought about the work in gold full of precious stones. The altar-piece is made up of 80 enamels which refer to episodes of Christ's life, of the Madonna and of Saint Mark. Here we note very beautiful images of angels, prophets, evangelists, and Emperors from the Orient. The Dome of the Presbytery is covered with a big mosaic with the figure of blessing Christ, the virgin among Prophets in the centre and in the vanes the symbols of the four Evangelists.

32. - ORIENTAL ARCH. Before the high altar is a marble balustrade on which rise eight columns surmounted by an architrave with fourteen statues: Saint Mark, the Virgin and the Twelve Apostles, which are the work of Iacobello and Pier Paolo dalle Masegne (1394). The bronze and silver Crucifix in the middle has been made by Iacopo di Marco Bennato. At the sides of the Presbytery are richly carved backs of chairs by Father Vincenzo dei Gesuiti and four tribunes for singers with mosaics representing the well known facts of the New Testament on the life of Jesus. They have been made from cartoons of Iacopo Tintoretto. From the Presbytery the Doge and other magistrates of the Republic used to observe the holy ceremonies.

33. - At the sides of the five little steps of the Presbytery, leaning on left and right pillars are the two pulpits or platforms; the one at the left of the Presbytery is a double pulpit of the XIV century, the inferior of octagonal shape and leaning on eleven columns of precious marbles, the superior for the Gospel, supported by seven little columns and covered with a little gilded bronze dome; the one at the right is the *pulpit of the relies* so called because it was here that the relics of Saints were shown in great religious celebrations. Moreover, from this pulpit the Doge was presented to the people following his election. It is poligonally shaped and is supported by nine columns of precious marbles. Above is the statue of the virgin attributed to Giovanni Bon.

34. - DOME OF THE ASCENSION: It presents an imposing mosaic (1200) of typical Byzantine taste with western influence which has as its subject « Christi in Glory » surrounded with flying angles, while below are the encircled Madonna and Apostles. Between the windows are the symbolical figures of the 16 virtues

which were the essential characteristics of living Christ. In the vanes are the four Evangelists and the four Sacred Rivers in the Bible.

35. - SOUTHERN ARCH: Here we can admire wonderful mosaics of the thirteenth century depicting the « Entrance of Jesus into Jerusalem », « Jesus Tempted », « The Last Supper », and the « Washing of the Feet ». At the centres « The Eternal Father in Glory », a work by Giacomo Pasterini of 1600.

36. - CHAPEL OF SAINT CLEMENT: Here also as in the Presbytery the chapel is preceded by a balustrade of red marble. Four columns support the architrave which is adorned with statues made by the Dalle Masegnas in 1397. On the altar is a bas-relief depicting the « Virgin » carved by Pirgotele in 1465. Right of the altar, from a window the Doge could attend the Mass without being seen. At the left is a reliquary with sculptures by the Dalle Masegnes. In the vaults are mosaics referring to the Fleeing of the Body of Saint Mark, the Departure from Alexandria in Egypt and the Arrival in Venice. Besides the organ other thirteenth century mosaics concerning Saint Clement's life are found here.

37. - ALTAR OF THE SACRAMENT: Before the altar let us note the two beautiful bronze chandeliers, the work of Maffeo Olivieri of 1527. At the right is a fifteenth century bas-relief with the figure of Saint Peter and the faithful, and on the other side is a Byzantine Madonna. Leaning against a pillar is an Angel in front of whom is lighted a lamp which commemorates the miraculous finding of the Body of Saint Mary. Here also are mosaics that represent Parables and Miracles of Jesus in the arch, while in the wall above the altar and between the windows are other mosaics representing episodes of Saint Leonard's life as this altar had been previously dedicated to this saint. Pietro Vecchia is the author of the cycle of mosaics.

38. - DOME OF SAINT LEONARDO: Mosaics of 1200 are found here representing much worshiped saints such as Saint Leonard, Nicholas, Biagio, Eufemia. Santa Tecla is by Vincenzo Bestiani (1512). In the little, exterior vault of the arch are other fifteenth century mosaics with figures of saints in the exterior one, around the great terracotta,

Baptistry: Baptismal Fount.

« Gothic Rose », opened in 1400, are other beautiful mosaics representing miracles of Christ by G. Pauletti. We must keep in mind that under the « Gothic Rose » is the door through which, the Doge used pass when entering the Basilica.

39. - RIGHT TRANSEPT: In the extreme rear is the entrance door to the Treasure; let us note on the door the arch of Moorish art of the XIII century. In the lunette between two Angels in mosaic is the little statue of the « Ecce Homo » of 1300; in the vaults of arches are, at the left, Saints Geminiano and Severo in mosaic.

40. - TREASURE OF SAINT MARK: It is preceded by a room called « Santuario »; here are kept precious reliquaries - it is estimated that there are 110 of them and other sacred objects. In the hall of the Treasure curios and precious are arranged insteand, objects which Venetians have succeeded in accumulating as spoils of war or in commercial dealings.

41. - RIGHT LATERAL NAVE: in the right wall are very beautiful mosaics of the Venetian school with Byzantine and Romanesque influence, having as a theme the « Praying Virgin and the Four Prophets » (1230). Beneath the last arcade has an enormous holy water stoup made of a porphyry basin entirely of one piece and decorated with Lombard sculptures.

42. - BAPTYSTERY: It is also called by the Venetian the « Church of the Putti » because of its baptismal function. This very beautiful place goes back to 1350, according to the wants of Doge Andrea Dandolo. This doge is buried here. The first thing that we notice is the Baptismal Font which has been designed by Iacopo Sansovino and perfectly realized with a fine artistic sense by Desiderio Fiorentino, Tiziano Minio and Francesco Segala.

Let us observe carefully the bronze cover which has the figures of the Evangelists and episodes of the life of Saint John. The little statue of the Saint is the work of Segala (1575). Before the altar is the tombal slab of Iacopo Sansovino and the « Paliotto » of gilded silver with figures of Saints; in the back are Byzantine bas-reliefs of 1200 and 1300 that represent the « Baptism of Christ » and Saints George and Theodore ». Here also we have vaults, large lunettes and domes decorated with fourteenth century mosaics. Those of the dome should be observed with interest:

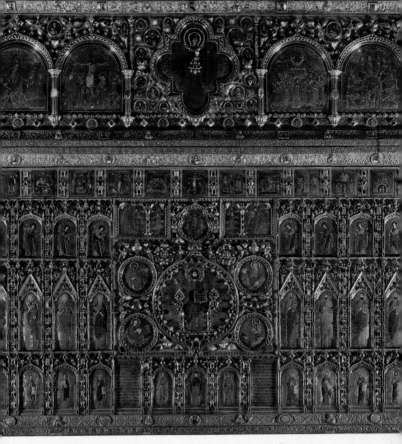

St. Mark's Basilica: The " Pala d'Oro " on the main altar.

« Christ and the Apostles Preaching the Gospel », the « Banquet of Herod », « Christ in Glory Surrounded by the Heavenly Powers » in the little cupola above the alter and « Episodes of the Life of the Baptist », and the « Crucifixion » in the big lunettes and in the walls.

43. - ZEN CHAPEL: The Republc decreed this splendid monument to Cardinal G. Battista Zen who, dying in 1501, left a rich legacy to the country. In the middle is the Tomb of the Cardinal cast in bronze, the work of Paolo Savin. The other sculptures and bronzes besides those by Savin have been made by Pietro Campanato; A. Leopardi and A. Lombardo. On the bronze altar is a bronze statue of the « Madonna della Scarpa » (Madonno of the Shoe), so called because a religious tradition

75

The Ducal Palace and the Campanile of St. Mark's.

tells us that a poor person gave his shoe to the Madonna as a gift and the shoe was miraculously changed into gold.

The fourteenth century mosaics tell of the life of Saint Mark and the main episodes of the contacts with the Venetian people. In the calotte of the apse is a « Madonna with Child between Angels ». At the walls is a Byzantine bas-relief with a Greek inscription representing the « Madonna ». Then let us also admire, between niches of Lombard style, the gracious little statues of the four prophets. At the sides let us note the two marble lions as well as a very beautiful « Christmas Scene » of Venetian-Romanesque style.

Going out the Basilica through the central doors of the hall, as we have noticed, by means of the littler door at the right we can go and visit the Marciano Museum which contains a stupendous series of works of art, especially arrases, rugs, and laces. Let us note the ancient organ, the work of Gentile Bellini, the ten arrases with episodes of the Passion of Jesus

View of the Ducal Palace.

made on designs by Zanino di Pietro, four arrases with
Stories of Saint Mark of 1551 made on designs by Sansovino, the polyptich painted by Paolo Veneziano ,a true masterpiece made in 1345, in which are represented Stories of
Saint Mark, Christ Deceased, Virgins and Saints. The polyptich in the past covered the golden altar-piece of the high
altar.

THE DUCAL PALACE

THE HISTORY. — If Rialto, at the beginning of Venetian fortunes,
was the social and commercial heart of Venice, it was here
that from the IX century the Government and Ducal headquarters
was established by Doges Angelo and Giustiniano Partecipazio.
It contains in itself the glory and the power of the Re-

public. Because the supreme Head of the State used to live in this magnificent residence, the building is called the Ducal palace. What we see at present has preserved nothing of its ancient appearance. It is well known that before the year one thousand, when it was built in Byzantine shape on pre-existing Roman walls, it was destroyed by a fire. Later it was many times rebuilt and, finally in 1340, in the full period of Gothic art, it was decided to rebuilt it and begin the construction facing the Basin along the breakwater and continuing with seven arches around the Little Square.

The architect who had planned this massive building is not yet known. What little tradition has told us is that the following contributed to its construction: Stone cutter Filippo Calendario, the « magister » porthus Palacii nove » Pietro Baseio and Proto Enrico. In 1400-1404 the facade towards the Lagoon with the large windows, was completed, the execution of which was entrusted to the Dalle Masegnes. In 1424 the part facing the Little Square was also completed.

Florentine and Milanese artists were called to complete the decoration of the imposing building; but the greatest part of the decorative complex in flowery Gothic was made by the components of the Bon family, all Venetians who could work in marble with exquisite artistic sense.

Thus was born this palace which knows no equal in the world: the ample arcades in the porch support the very gracious loggia made more precious by a beautiful tunnel. Above is developed the clear facade from the appropriate lozenge polychrome design in which are the ogival openings of the large windows. To interrupt harmoniously the flat surface of the facade Iacobello and Pier Paolo Dalle Masegne, in 1404, built the central balcony which is also repeated in the front of the Piazzetta, while the whole building is crowned by white battlements.

WORK OF ART:

EXTERNAL FACADE. — Let us begin the visit from the facade which faces the Basin and precisely to the Straw Bridge which crosses the Palace Rio, so called on account of the third facade which is prospected here. We know that this part was planned by Architect Antonio Rizzo (1430-1498). Let us admire the powerful architectural conception of this artist who has been able to give the construction an austere and solemn Renaissance form, not in contrast with the Byzantine-Venetian tradition.

Looking at the facade on the mole we are struck by the very beautiful parapet of flowery Gothic style by the Dalle Masegnes. At one time to this parapet was added the statue of Venice and above the symbols of Justice which are the works of Alessandro Vittoria, the most famous sculptor in the end of the XVI century. On should also note the porch (measuring on this side

Ducal Palace: Porta della Carta.

71,50 meters and having 17 arcades) which was buried at one time. It is calculated that it sinks for about 40 cm., thus we can imagine the architectural effect and the original luminosity. The beauty of the porch is rendered more precious by the capitals which compete with those of the loggias. Many of them have been remade and substituted with copies. They have been made at various periods by Lombard, Venetian and Tuscan artists who put to it all their sculptural and plastic capacities. These capitals constitute a remarcable series of allegorical, conographical and decorative representations which are rarely found in other buildings of this kind.

Even those having little time should not forget to admire the relief at the corners of the construction: the one facing the Straw Bridge represents « The Drunkness of Noah », a sculpture having a rude fourteenth century realistic sense; above are the figures of « Tobia and Archangel Raphael »; the one at the corner of the Piazzetta is « Adam and Eve », a work that goes back to the beginning of the fifteenth century and contains a plastic impostation which is little mature. The capitals of the porch of the Piazzetta (here the porch is 75 meters long and 18 arches) repeat the motifs of the main facade. In the middle is the parapet) made by pupils of Sansovino in 1536 in imitation of the other one on the Mole. Let us note the figure of Doge Andrea Gritti before the symbol of Venice (a recent reconstruction by U. Bottasso); at the summit of the parapet is the statue of « Justice » by Alessandro Vittoria, the sculptures in the niches are the work of Danese Cattaneo and Pietro da Salo. At the corner, near the Door of Paper, above the capital of Justice, is the big marble relief called « The Judgment of Salomon » a live, human work rendered with beautiful plastic and colouristic effects. It is attributed to Nanni di Bartolo il Rosso (the Red) or to the Florentine School of the Lambertis.

La Porta della Carta. — Once it was gilded and it got this name from the fact that it was here where the decress of the Republic were posted. A wonderful arch enriched by a well ordered polichrome disposition of carvings and decorative elements of Gothic taste makes this Door the worthy access into the Ducal Palace. Here worked Giovanni and Bartolomeo Bon (1438). Although not the whole decoration follows a homogeneous line, the work has a superlative artistic value. Of no-

Ducal Palace: The Courtyard.

table beauty are the figures of « Virtues » located in the niches of the pillars, and representing « Temperance, Fortitute, Charity and Prudence » On the portal is « Doge Francesco Foscari before the Winged Lion », a modern work in substitution of that of the same subject which was destroyed during the revolutionary events of 1797.

It is the work of L. Ferrari made in 1885. Above the window three lights, in the tondo, is « Saint Mark », at the summit of the pinnacle is the statue of « Justice ».

Ducal Palace: The Staircase of the Giants.

INTERIOR OF THE DUCAL PALACE

THE COURTYARD. — From the Porta della Carta we enter the hall which shows to visitors the coat - of - arms of Doge Francesco Foscari. From here we can go into the spacious and very beautiful courtyard. The first thing which calls the tourist's attention is the Eastern facade, before the entrance which is the work of Antonio Rizzo (1483-98). The beauty of this facade is the marvelous solution realized by the architect who has been able to harmonize the Gothic style of the construction in the inferior portion, by inserting Renaissance forms in the upper portion thus creating an architectural masterpiece in line with Venetian architectural characteristics. The facade is a little too decorative and disturbs the whole of the building. This decoration, which has its particular kind of plastic beauty, is due to Pietro Lombardo, Giorgio Spavento and Scarpagnino who brought to completion the southern part of the facade. The two facades in red bricks and inspired to the external, decorative motifs of the Palace and which close the courtyard from the Western and Eastern sides are by Bartolomeo Manopola. In the middle of the courtyard are two beautiful bronzes. The first towards the Foscari arcade is by Alfonso Alberghetti (1559) decorated with coat-of-arms and caryatids; the other by Nicolò dei Conti (1556) which has depicted Doge Francesco Falier and « The Miracle of the Holy Water ».

In the facade of the Clock which leans against the Foscari arcade at the North let us note in the niches the six ancient restored statues, the construction is of Baroque style with two orders of round arches in the porch and pointed arches in the loggia. It is the work of Bartolomeo Monopola of 1614. On the right side is the statue of Francesco Mari I della Rovere, the Duke of Urbino, by the Florentine G. Bandini (1587). Let us now take a look at the Foscari arch, in front of the Staircase of the Giants. It is here shown in all its architectural beauty. Rizzo and Bregno in Renaissance forms. Here also the two styles are perfectly combined and harmonious; let us note the statue of Saint Mark and other allegorical figures, in the niches below we see two copies in bronze depicting « Adam » and « Eve » the originals of which in marble, true masterpieces made by Rizzo, we see the Ducal apartment. At the side of the Staircase of the Giants is the hall of the Senators, so called because it seems that they gathered here to attend solemn ceremonies. The facade of this side, with its beautiful and elegant windows, has been made in collaboration with Architects Scarpagino and Spavento at the beginning of 1500.

In front of the Foscari Arch is the *Staircase of the Giants.* It took this name from the two enormous statues of « Mars » and « Mercury » sculptured by Sansovino and his helpers. Architect Rizzo has been here particularly clever in realizing this bold and solemn choice, by putting in relief even in the decorations those plastic values which are his own and which obey to a high concept of grandeur which is most appro-

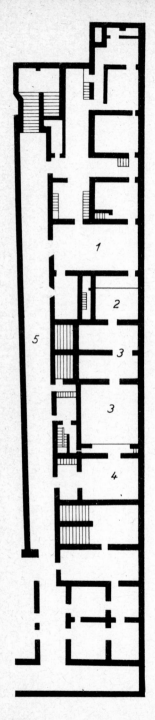

FIRST FLOOR

1) Ducal Chancellery
2) Office of the Marine Police
3) Halls of Avogaria
4) Hall of Censors
5) Golden Staircase

Ducal Palace: The Golden Staircase (detail).

priate to the glorious Republic. In fact, at the summit of the flight of stairs, in the presence of dignitaries and of the people, the Doge was crowned; from here, assisted by his court, he received illustrious guests and ambassadors.

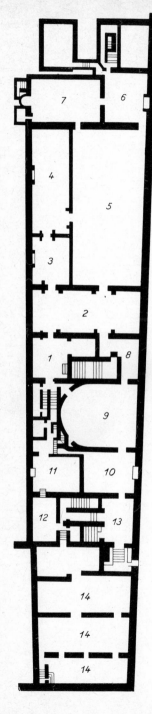

THIRD FLOOR

1) Square Hall
2) Hall of the Four Doors
3) Antecollege
4) Hall of the College
5) Hall of the Senate
6) Antechurch
7) The Little Church
8) Corridor
9) Hall of the Council of the Ten
10) Hall of the Compass
11) Hall of the Heads of the Council of the Ten
12) Room of the Inquisitors
13) Landing of the Staircase of the Censors
14) Hall of Arms of the Council of the Ten

FIRST FLOOR

1. - DUCAL CHANCELLERY: In this room, which was once Office of the Chancellor who was nominated for life as was the Doge, one can now purchase tickets for the visit to the palace.

2. - OFFICE OF THE MARINE POLICE: This was the headquarters of those whose task it was to reclute young people for the military service in the navy Among the works of art let us note on the door « The Queen of Saba » of the School of Ricci; « Venice and Saint Mark » by Liberi and an « Adoration of the Magi » by A. Celesti.

3. - HALLS OF AVOGARIA: The Avogaria was a magistrature which administered Justice, guarded the municipal register, the golden book in which were proofs of Venetian nobility and that of Silver for families of citizens. In the first hall are « Portraits of Avogadri » by Donato Veneziano (1459), an « Annunciation » by Palma the Younger, the « Christ among the Clouds » by Domenico Tintoretto and other portraits by eighteenth century artists. In the second hall (here gathered the Tribunal, the room was then in direct communication with the Prisons through the Bridge of Sighs) a « Pietà » the early work of Giovanni Bellini, a masterpiece by Iacopo Tintoretto « Resurrection with three Avogradi », a « Madonna » and « portraits » by Leandro Bassano.

4. - HALL OF CENSORE: Here had their office the Censors whose duty was to watch on the customs of the nobility and to report electoral plots. Let us note around the walls the coat-of-arms of 266 Censors (from 1317 to 1629). Moreover we have here portraits of several Censors due to Domenico Tintoretto, Paolo de Franceschi and Palma Antonio. Coming from the left is the Staircase of the Censors.

5. - GOLDEN STAIRCASE: It has this name on account of the marvelous decoration in gilded stuccos made by Alessandro Vittoria. It was built on a design by Iacopo Sansovino between 1523-38 and finished in 1559. By means of this staircase we have access into the Ducal apartment and to the halls of the third floor. The frescos that we see are by G.B. Franco, the sculptures « Hercules » and « Atlas » by I. Aspetti. At the third floor we see « Abundance and Charity » a statue by Francesco Segala. In order to have a systematic view of the several halls, it is advisable to go up the Golden Staircase as far as the third floor, from which, then, through the Staircase of the Censors, we shall go down to the second.

THIRD FLOOR

1. - SQUARE HALL: In the wooden ceiling is one of the most beautiful works by Iacopo Tintoretto. On an octagonal cloth is painted the scene of « Doge Jerome Priuli receiving from Justice the sword and the scale in the presence of Peace and of Saint Jerome », a bold composition of great colouristc and perspective effect. At the walls are various paintings among which we note those by Paolo Veronese « Adam and Eve » and « Praying in the Orchard ».

2. - HALL OF THE FOUR DOORS: It was at one time the headquarters of the College and has later become the antechamber of honour to the hall of the Senate. The architecture has been made after a design by Andrea Palladio by Antonio da Ponte, decorations and stuccos in white and gold, paintings in the ceiling, at the walls are painted cloths and allegorical statues. The whole is a hymn to the power of Venice .Among the many works we will cite the most important: in the ceiling are the stuccos of G.B. Candi called Bombarda and the « Triumphs of Venice » by Iacopo Tintoretto; « Doge Antonio Grimani

Ducal Palace: To the left: **Hall of the Antecollege;**
above: " **Neptune offering Venice the gifts of the Sea** ", by Tiepolo.

worshiping Faith and Saint Mark » by Titian; in the big
window overlooking the lagoon is a cloth by G. B. Tiepolo
representing « Neptune offering to Venice the gifts of the
Sea ».

3. - ANTECOLLEGE: Here used to wait the great personalities
waiting to be received by the Doge. In the ceiling is a restored
fresco by Veronese « Venice Distributing Honours and Com-
pensations ». The imposing chimney was made on a design
by Vincenzo Scamozzi, while the sculptures are by Tiziano
Aspetti, the frieze in stucco is by Vittoria. Let us admire now
the four textiles by Tintoretto: on the entrance wall « Vulcano's
Forge and Mercury and Graces », on the one in front « Bacchus and Ariadna » and « Minerva kicks Mars out ». These
are stupendous masterpieces of this great master of colour.
On the wall in front of the windows is a famous work by
Paolo Veronese « Rape of Europe, somewhat altered by numerous improvements.

4. - HALL OF THE COLLEGE: Here the Doge, helped by the high
magistrates, used to discuss affairs of State and gave audiences.
The architecture is by Da Ponte on designs by Pelladio and
Rusconi. The ceiling is the decorative work of Francesco
Bello (1577). In the sections are paintings by Veronese, a very
beautiful pictorial, allegorical cycle full of luminosity and
compositive grace. They represent: at the centre « Allegory of
Faith », below « Ancient Sacrifice », above the tribune « Venice in throne honoured by Justice and Peace », above the
entrance « Mars and Neptune » and all around the figures
« Prosperity, Fidelity, Vigilance, Gentleness, Dialectics, Simplicity, Compensation, and Moderation ». Above the tribunal,
always by Veronese: « Exaltation of the Victory of Lepanto ».
The other textiles adorning the hall and the subjects of which
are figures of Doges with religious and allegorical attributes,
are works by the great Tintoretto.

5. - HALL OF THE SENATE: In this large hall used to take place meetings of senators presided by the Doge and other high magistates. The pictorial decoration is an exaltation of divine satisfaction towards the Republic, of its civilization and government.

The main work are: in the ceiling, designed by Christopher Sorte (1580), the great painting by Tintoretto « Venice, the Queen of the Sea »; above the throne of the Doge, always by Tintoretto, « Dead Christ » and the cloth with « Doge Loredan praying the Virgin to end the famine and to give victory over the Turks »; on the door before the throne « Doges Lorenzo and Girolamo Priuli praying the Redeemer for the liberation of Venice from famine and from pestilence » is the work of Palma the Younger. The Senatorial seats were renewed in the XVIII century.

6. - ANTICHIESETTA (ANTECHURCH): It is decorated with stuccos. In the ceiling are frescos by Iacopo Guarana representing « Allegories of a good Government »; in the walls the cartoons which Sebastiano Ricci prepared for the mosaic of the facade of the Basilica of San Marco. Their subject matter is « Saint Mark's Body worshiped at his arrival in Venice, by the Signoria ».

7. - THE LITTLE CHURCH: Architecture by Vincenzo Scamozzi (1593). On the Altar is a « Madonna and Child and San Giovannino », an expressive sculpture by Iacopo Sansovino. In the ceiling are frescos by Iacopo Guarena and pictorial by Mengozzi Colonna .

8. - CORRIDOR: We get here by crossing the hall of the Senate and that of the Four Doors. Let us note on the walls works by Gerolamo Bosch. They represent « Hell »; « Paradise »; the tryptych.

Temptations of Saints Jerome, Anthony and Egidio hermits; that of the « Martyrdom of Saint Giuliana ». The imaginative and macabre Flemish painter has here manifested all his narrative ability with satyrical vivacity.

9. - COUNCIL OF THE TEN: Here used to hold its meetings the most feared Venetian Magistrature. It was made up of ten members and watched over the security of the State. The pictorial decoration imply the qualities which were to inspire the members of the Council. The most important works are in the ceiling: in the central part « Zeus lightnening vices » is a copy of the original painting by Veronese which was taken by the French in 1797, now at the Louvre Museum.

Always by the same artist let us note « The old Oriental and the Young Woman »; and Juno offering Venice the Ducal Horn ». In the other sections are allegorical painting by G. B. Ponchino and G. B. Zelotti, while by Veronese are (in the ceiling with gilded sculptures) sixteen little paintings in chiaroscuro. In the walls is a frieze with paintings by Zelotti, « Pope Alexander III, Barbarossa and Doge Ziani » by F. L. da Ponte; the « Adoration of the Magi » by Aliense and « The Peace of Bologna of 1529 by M. Vecelio.

10. - HALL OF THE COMPASS: It takes this name from the double door which leads into the near Hall of the Heads of the Council of the Ten. Here used to stop the condemned people and those who were watched by the State Police. In the wall let us observe the famous « Mouth of a Lion » which used to serve for secret denunciations. The chimney is the work of Sansovino and his helpers (1554). In the ceiling we see a copy of a painting by Veronese which is now found at the Louvre and which represents « Saint Mark and the Virtues ». Original

Ducal Palace: Above: " The Rape of Europe " by Veronese;
below: " The Three Graces ", by Tintoretto.

Ducal Palace: Bacchus, Ariadne and Venus, by Tintoretto.

by the same painter are the eighteen paintings in chiaroscuro. At the walls are « Surrender of Bergamo and Surrender of Brescia » by Aliense.

11) HALL OF THE HEADS OF THE COUNCIL OF TEN: The pictorial decoration alludes to the duties of the Council of the Ten. By Veronese is « The Punishment of the Forger » on the entrance door; and on the side of the windows « Subdued Sin of Victory ». The Chimney is by Sansovino. At the walls are notable works of art among which: « Madonna » by the Cremonese Boccaccino, « Dead Christ » by Antonello da Saliba, Christ among the Jews » by Metsys.

12. - ROOM OF THE INQUISITORS: He who committed political crimes or acts against the securithy of the State was questioned here. The room was adjoined to the prisons. The paintings of the ceiling are by Tintoretto and represent « Faith, Fortitude, Beneficence; and the Prodigal Son ».

13. - LANDING OF THE STAIRCASE OF THE CENSORS: We arrive at the landing by going through the Hall of the Chiefs of the Council of the Ten and from the Hall of the Compass, from here through a little staircase we enter the Halls of Arms.

14. - HALLS OF ARMS OF THE COUNCIL OF THE TEN: In the past these places also acted as prisons, but since the beginning of the XIV century they were used as a weapons room. Today they contain a well-ordered and interesting collection of arms of the past centuries. Big swords, picks, halberds; arquebus, culverin; the armour of Henry the IV of France, two armouries

92

SECOND FLOOR

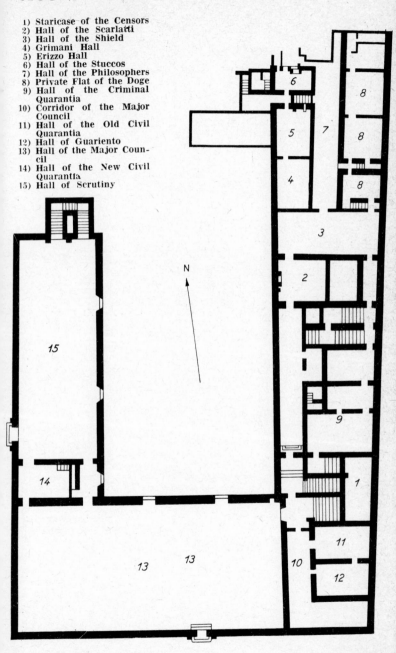

belonging to the Sforza family, an arquebus with twenty barrels and a beautiful Venetian sword finely engraved of the XIV century. Among the works of sculpture the bust in marble of Sebastian Venier, the Hero of Lepanto, sculptured by Alessandro Vittoria, that in bronze by Francesco Morosini the work of the Genovese Filiberto Parodi, that in bronze Marcantonio Bragadini by Tiziano Aspetti.

SECOND FLOOR

- HALL OF THE CENSORS: Going down this staircase we shall be back at the second floor and thus in the apartment of the Doge to which we can get by crossing a long Gallery.

2. - HALL OF THE SCARLATTI: It is so called because it was here where used to gather those who were part of the following of the Doge and used to wear scarlet-coloured togas The very beautiful ceiling decorated in gold on a blue background is by Biagio and Pietro da Faenza (1505. By Antonio and Arturo Lobardo the chimney with the Barbarigo coat-of-arms; of notable artistic merit is the stucco « Madonna and Child » of the Paduan School, the bas-relief « Doge Leonardo Loredana recommended to the Virgin by San Marco, Saint Leonard and another Saint » is attributed to Pietro Lombardo ».

3. - HALL OF THE SHIELD: It is so called because here used to be kept the shield belonging to the last Doge Ludovico Manin (1789-97). Moreover here used to stop the Guard of the Doge. The geographical maps were made in 1762 by F. Grisellini working on the previously existing ones of 1540.

4. - Grimani Hall: In the ceiling is the coat-of-arms of the family which gives its name to the hall, around is a frieze with symbolical figures attributed to Andrea Vicentino, the marble chimney has been made at the beginning of 1500 by Tullio and Antonio Lombardo. By Vittorio Carpaccio is the painting « Lion of Saint Mark ». Let us note the « Head in marble of Doge Francesco Foscari » sculptured by B. Bon, and which belonged to the relief on the Door of the Court, which was destroyed in 1797.

5. - Erizzo Hall: The coat-of-arms on the chimney of Doge Erizzo gives the name to the hall. The engraved ceiling is of the XVI century. The beautiful « Lion of Saint Mark » is the signed work of Iacobello del Fiore; the frieze with putti by G.B. Lorenzetti. From the terrace, reduced to a garden, is a beautiful view of the courtyard.

6. - HALL OF THE STUCCOS: It is so called on account of the stuccos decorating it which go back to the Dogeship of Marino Grimani. On the chimney is a coat-of-arms by Lorenzo Priuli. In this hall we can admire the beautiful paingings by Bonifacio Pitati: « Adoration of the Magi ». By Tintoretto « Portrait of Henry II »; by Leandro Bassano « Adoration of the Shepherds », by Giuseppe Porta called Salviati « Holy Family ».

7. - HALL OF THE PHILOSOPHERS: It is so called on account of the twelve philosophers painted by Tintoretto and Veronese and now transferred to the Library. Through the long corridor and across a hall we can enter the private chapel of the Doge. On the door is a masterpiece by Tiziano « San Cristoforo ».

Ducal Palace: Hall of the College.

Ducal Palace: Hall of the Senate.

8. - PRIVATE FLAT OF THE DOGE: We can enter it from the other side of the corridor of the philosophers. The first room is supposed to have been the bedroom, in the second is to be noted a beautiful chimney of Lombardesque style; in the third Tullio and Antonio Lombardo have made the very beautiful chimney with an allegorical frieze.

9. - HALL OF THE CRIMINAL QUARANTIA: From the Doge's flat through a long corridor we reach the Hall of Quarantia, the headquarters of the inquisitor magistrates. It is divided into two rooms, in the first we find the statues of Adam and in the second that of Eve. Here are the originals in marble which were once located in the Foscari Arch and which have been brought here to protect them from the damages of time. They can be considered real masterpieces by Antonio Rizzo who, through these two works, has been able to gain the first place in Venetian sculptorial art. Let us note the powerful virile expression of Adam and the grace emanating from the body of Eve, and from their face radiates a great many sentiments, the true reflection of the acknowledgment of her guilt with a malicious complacency. Once we are out of the Criminal Quarantia let us return to the Censors' Hall to see the rooms that lead into the Hall of the Major Council.

Ducal Palace: Hall of the " Bussola ".

10. - CORRIDOR OF THE MAJOR COUNCIL: It is a corridor with beautiful Gothic windows which face the Molo. It used to be the entertainment centre for the mobles during the intervals of the sessions of the Maggior Consiglio. At the walls can be noted: at the right works by Palma the Younger, at the left paintings by Tintoretto. Both artists have sought to exalt the two Doges and to depict symbolical figures referring to cities of the Venetian empire in the terra firma.

11. - HALL OF THE OLD CIVIL QUARANTIA: It was the headquarters of a supreme court composed of forty members who were in charge of civil matters and of the city's possessions. Let us note: « Moses Causing the Golden Calf to be Destroyed » and « Moses Punishes the Idolaters » by Antonio Celesti; « Annunciation », « The people directed towards Venice in throne », « Mercury, the god of commerce, leads the prisoners », three works by P. Malombra; « Venice receives the sceptre of leadership » by G.B. Lorenzetti and in the capital « Madonna in throne » by an anonymous author of the fifteenth century.

12. - HALL OF GUARIENTO: In the past here used to be kept ammunitions. As a matter of fact it was called « hall of weapons ». Here is kept a famous work by the Paduan Guariento: « Paradise » which he had painted for the Hall of the Major Council.
Now we can only see fragments because after the fire of 1577 it was greatly damaged and substituted by the work of the same subject by Tintoretto. Yet, the following are to be admired: « Crowning of the Virgin » Saints, Prophets, Angels and Beati.

13. - HALL OF THE MAJOR COUNCIL: It is an imposing and spacious room in which were held meetings of the Major Council. It is 15.40 meters high, 25 wide and 54 long. On the mole are five Gothic windows, two on the little square and two on the courtyard. From each of these imposing windows one can enjoy suggestive views of the sea and of the monuments which crown the mole of the palace. After the fire of 1557 - which destroyed the room inaugurated in 1423 by Doge Francesco Foscari, and during which were destroyed the famous paintings of the major Venetian painters - the hall was rebuilt by Antonio da Ponte and decorated as we see it now with subjects suggested by the Florentine Girolamo de' Bardi and by the Venetian historian F. Sansovino.
The first thing which strikes us is the immense textile over the Tribune which represents « Paradise » the work of Tintoretto (1590). Its measurements are 7x22 meters.
When the artist made this oil painting he was 70 years old and was helped by his son Domenico. It has undergone numerous restorations which have lessened its great original chiaroscural effects. Still to be admired, however, is the monumentality of the composition with the Virgin and Christ at the centre and Saints all around. The second point of attraction for the visitor is the very beautiful ceiling by Cristoforo Sorte made between 1578 and 1584 during the Dogeship of Niccolò da Ponte. It is made up of large gilded and carved cornices which divide the space of the ceiling into thirty-five zones. Let us now look at the main works of the

Ducal Palace: Hall of the three Chefs of the Council of Ten.

ceiling by turning our shoulders to the Tribune and beginning from those towards the wall of the mole. Once arrived at the end we shall go towards the Tribune by passing in the middle of the hall, then we shall pass to the right flank to arrive at the door of the New Civil Quarantia. First section: « Antonio Loredana directs the attack to free Scutari from the siege of Mohamed II » by Paolo Veronese. Second section: The Venetian army and navy take by storm Polesella (1482-84) by Francesco Bassano. Third: « Victore Soranzo with his fleet defeats at Argenta (1482) the armies of Hercules I of Este » by Iacopo Tintoretto and helpers. Fourth: « Iacopo Marcello conquers Gallipoli (1494) » by Tintoretto. Fifth: « Giorgio Cornaro and Bartolomeo d'Alviano defeat in Cadore the imperials of Maximillian I (1508) » by Francesco Bassano. Sixth: Andrea Gritti reconquers Padua (1510) by Palma the Younger. Seventh: in the oval section « Venice crowned by Victory welcomes the conquered people and provinces surrounding its throne » by Palma the Younger. Eighth: in the great rectangle « Venice surrounded by the sea divinities gives a branch of olive to Doge Niccolò da Ponte who presents to the city the respects of the Senate and the gifts of the subject provinces » by Iacopo Tintoretto and helpers. Ninth: in the oval section « Apotheosis of Venice surrounded by divinities and crowned by Glory » by Paolo Veronese. Tenth (side of the courtyard): « Pietro Mocenigo fighting in Smirne against the Turks 1471 » by Paolo Veronese. Eleventh: « Michele Attendolo leads the Venetians to victory in Casalmaggiore » (1446) by Francesco Bassano Twelvth: « Stefano Contarini is victorious in Riva against the fleet of the Visconti (1440) » by Iacopo Tintoretto and helpers. Thirteenth: « Venetians led by Francesco Barbaro help the Brescians to break the siege of Filippo Visconti (1438) » by Iacopo Tintoretto. Fourteenth: « Campagnola leads Venetians to victory in Maclodio (1426) » by Francesco Bassano. Fifteenth: « Francesco Bembo with the fleet of Po conquers the Viscontis at Cremona » by Palma the Younger.

Since our eyes are turned towards the ceiling; let us note at the top of the walls the frieze with the series of portraits of the Doges made by Domenico Tintoretto and helpers. It begins at the middle of the wall towards the courtyard, let us note one where there is no portrait at all, but only a black textile painted with a writing in Latin which reads as follows: « This is the place of Marin Faliero, beheaded on account of his crimes ». The paintings towards the courtyard refer to episodes of the fight between Pope Alexander III against Federigo Barbarossa to which participated only politically Venice. They are by several authors, but from the artistic point of view let us admire the fourth section (moving from the end of the hall) « Ambassadors ask for peace to Barbarossa » from the School of Tintoretto; the fifth « the Pope handing the key to the Doge » the tenth, « Federigo Barbarossa prostrated before the Pope » by Federigo Zuccari.

On the wall facing the Molo the paintings describe facts of che Fourth Crusade led by Doge Enrico Dandolo. These sceness have been painted by minor painters. On the back wall, opposite « Paradise » let us note a painting by Veronese « The return of Doge Contarini after victory in Chioggia ».

14. - HALL OF THE NEW CIVIL QUARANTIA: Here used to reside the tribunal of appeal for the subjects of terra firma. Let us ·note the beautiful ceiling with gilded beams of the year 1500. Above the tribune is a wall covered with gilded leather and having the coats-of-arms of judges, high above is the « Madonna » on a background and of the fifteenth century. At the

walls, « Venice and Justice » by A. Foler, « Venice and Neptune », the « Virtues » and « Justice chasing Vices » by G.B. Lorenzetti, « Justice and Time revealing Truth » by F. Zaniberti.

15. - HALL OF SCRUTINY: From 1532 were held here the scrutinies for the voting of the Major Council and here used to gather the commissioners for the election of the Doge. Before the fire of 1577 there used to be at the walls paintings by Tintoretto and Pordenone. The hall was restored in 1587 by Antonio da Ponte. For this large room also adopted a pictorial decoration suggested by learned men who were preoccupied to exalt the maritime undertakings of Venice. Among the numerous works of art we shall cite the most important ones. In the ceiling (rich of engraved and gilded cornices, attributed to Sorte) « The taking of Padua » by Francesco Bassano who makes himself admired on account of the varied tones of colour; on the entrance wall « The Universal Judgment » by Palma the Younger; on that towards the courtyard « The conquest of Zara » by Tintoretto and helpers. Above the windows Andrea Vicentino narrates « The Day in Lepanto ». On top of the walls is the series of portraits of the Doges begun in the Hall of the Major Council. From the balcony we enjoy a splendid view over the little square and the square with the Basilica.

In the back of the hall is the imposing Arch of Triumph in honour of Doge Francesco Morosini, an architectural imitation of classical-Roman style attributed to Antonio Tirali. Past the Arch of Triumph is the Staircase of the Ccrutiny which takes to the first floor and then, through a corridor at the right, introduces us into the splendid Foscara Loggia of which is to be admired the architecure and all that is magnificent on the little square and beyond, especially the unforgettable vision which one has of the Basin of Saint Mark once one reached the south-western corner. Going again along the Foscara Loggia, at its end, we can enter the loggias which face courtyard. Here we see the marble busts representing illustrious Venetian men. In the right wall several doors lead into the the ancient offices of the Republic.

THE PRISONS: In the eastern arm of the Loggias, near the Scala d'Oro, through a little door we can visit the Prisons and the Bridge of Sighs wich was connected with the Avogaria and other Tribunals.

The bridge of Sighs was used to bring before the judges the prisoners. The latter, looking through the windows, could see portion of the Laguna and sigh for the lost freedom as well as for the anxiety produced by the questioning and the process. This state of mind gave the name to the bridge. Before the building of the Palace of the Prisons, these were called Old Prisons and were divided into two particular sections: the *Piombi* (Leads) where were located the cells under the roof covered with lead, so that the prisoners suffered hot and cold weather at their most intense state, and the *Pozzi* (wells) placed at the ground floor and destined to those guilty of greater crimes. By going down a little ladder one can see the 18 cells of the Pozzi. Only one cell, preserved as it was at the beginning, make us understand the possible state of the condemned men closed in those « pozzi ».

Two picturesque streets near Piazza San Marco.

THE GRAND CANAL

The Grand Canal: the wonder of Venice, of Italy and of the world. An immense vein of water produces a peculiar « S » which divides the city into two parts. An « S » which is about 3.800 meters long with a width which varies from 30 to 70 meters and with a depth of about five and a half meters. It is indeed a marvelous artery with its wavy, clear and serene surface which is now foamy, now dark according to the humour of the sky, of the seasons and of men's vitality. The great waterway presents itself to the visitor with the green cupola of San Simone Piccolo and here and there in the opposite banks are seen in all their spectacular magnificence rii, palaces, fields, foundations that impress our imagination; the human eye is not capable of grasping everything, lost and amazed by that splendid sequence which changes continually its appearance, its colouring; it assumes a massive consistence on account of the beautiful and impressive luxury houses which are scattered everywhere to remind us of various architectural epochs.

Yet, it's not only our senses which want fulfillment, but also our mind and heart. And even the most superficial glance can carry such an impact as to overwhelm our emotions: the small fields dotting pictorially into the the water, the humble little houses, the deep burrows of the rii, the short and green walls of a garden, the leafy portion of a tree jotting out into the canal, the people who give a sense of newness to the small foundations, the slow and careful gliding of the gondolas, the corpulent arrogance of the big cargo boats, the traffic of motorboats and little boats agitating the waters and rippling them and making them foamy and sending them to break against and flood and corroding the darkened steps of palaces, of houses and docking platforms.

How many palaces and souvenirs does the Canal Grande contain! We shall only speak of the most important ones, of the bridges, of the most famous personalities who along this lively course of water admired, lived and worked inspired by that delicate poetry and beauty which took in abundance from this waterway. To understand the wonderful admiration of Filippo di Commynes, the French ambassador of the fifteenth century, of Herman Melville, the great navigator and writer who visited it in 1857, of King Henry the III of France who was here splendidly received in 1574, of George Byron, of Robert Browning, of Richard Wagner, Canova, Foscolo who all lived here in the eighteenth century until the period of d'Annunzio, to mention just the greatest names, it will be necessary to feel that transcendental atmosphere which lives and personifies itself along the Grand Canal. Writers, poets, musicians, painters, sculptors, playwriters felt, each according to their geniuses, this atmosphere which gave them new capacities, genial intuitions, sensibilities till then unknown, a necessary complement and a contribution to the highest expression in their masterpieces.

To this contributed to a great extent the changing character of the Grand Canal according to the season of the year.

With a dark or cloudy sky, clear and brilliant with the sun, calm and serene, dark or shining with the moon, hazy or rainy, there is no way of escaping that particular atmosphere that reveals the most unthought of objects, which gives relief to architectural works, form the immense play of lights and shadows which projects reality into the fictitious, the sudden change in colour of the gigantic forms shine and move reflected in the water, made to look trembling and fragile by the now slow now caressing and then aggressive and menacing flow of the waters: they also are capable of giving the most interesting and colourful images. All this is the Canal Grande; not only for the most sensitive people, but also for the simple folks who arrive here to understand such magnificence with that « oh » of wonder which comes out spontaneously and lasts and infinitum before such dream-like vision.

BEGINNING FROM SAINTS MARK'S TO THE STATION, LOOKING TO THE RIGHT

CA' GIUSTINIAN - Gothic building from 1474, actually in propriety of the municipality and houses the municipal offices and the Biennale d'Arte.

PALAZZO CONTARINI-FASSAN - Also called « Casa di Desdemona », was built in 1475 in gothic Style with clear Renaissance influence in the decorative elements.

Ca' Grande.

PALAZZO CORNER DELLA CA' GRANDE - Now seat of the Prefecture, it is the largest palace on the Canal Grande. A work of Sansovino (1537) it was built on the area of the pre-existing palace Malombra burnt down in 1532.

PALAZZO CAVALLI, NOW FRANCHETTI - Built originally in the XV century, rebuilt in 1890. Noteworthy is the facade for the rich decorations of the central windows.

Academy Bridge.

ACADEMY BRIDGE - Temporary wooden construction
with a single arch. It is the first of the three bridges
that cross the Canal.

PALAZZETTO FALIER - Characteristic gothic construction of the XV century with two lateral loggias.

PALAZZO GRIMANI - Stupendous renaissance building
with three floors and wide arches. Masterpiece of
the XVI century by the architect Michele Sanmicheli.
Actually seat of the Court.

Palazzo Cavalli-Franchetti.

The Rialto Bridge.

The Warehouse of the Germans.

RIALTO BRIDGE

48 metres long, 22 wide and 7,50 high. Artistically this heavy and massive construction is not in harmony with the architecture surrounding it, however, it is the most famous and majestic bridge in Venice. It was begun in 1588 by Antonio da Ponte and completed in 1592. Each head rests on 6.000 poles. Above, almost always crowded, it is divided into three flights of steps, and double arcades, occupied by shops, flank the central flight. From the two parapets, there is a fine view of the Grand Canal,

FONDACO DEI TEDESCHI - (now central post office), renaissance building by Scarpagnini (1505). Once the facade was decorated with frescoes by Giorgione and Titian.

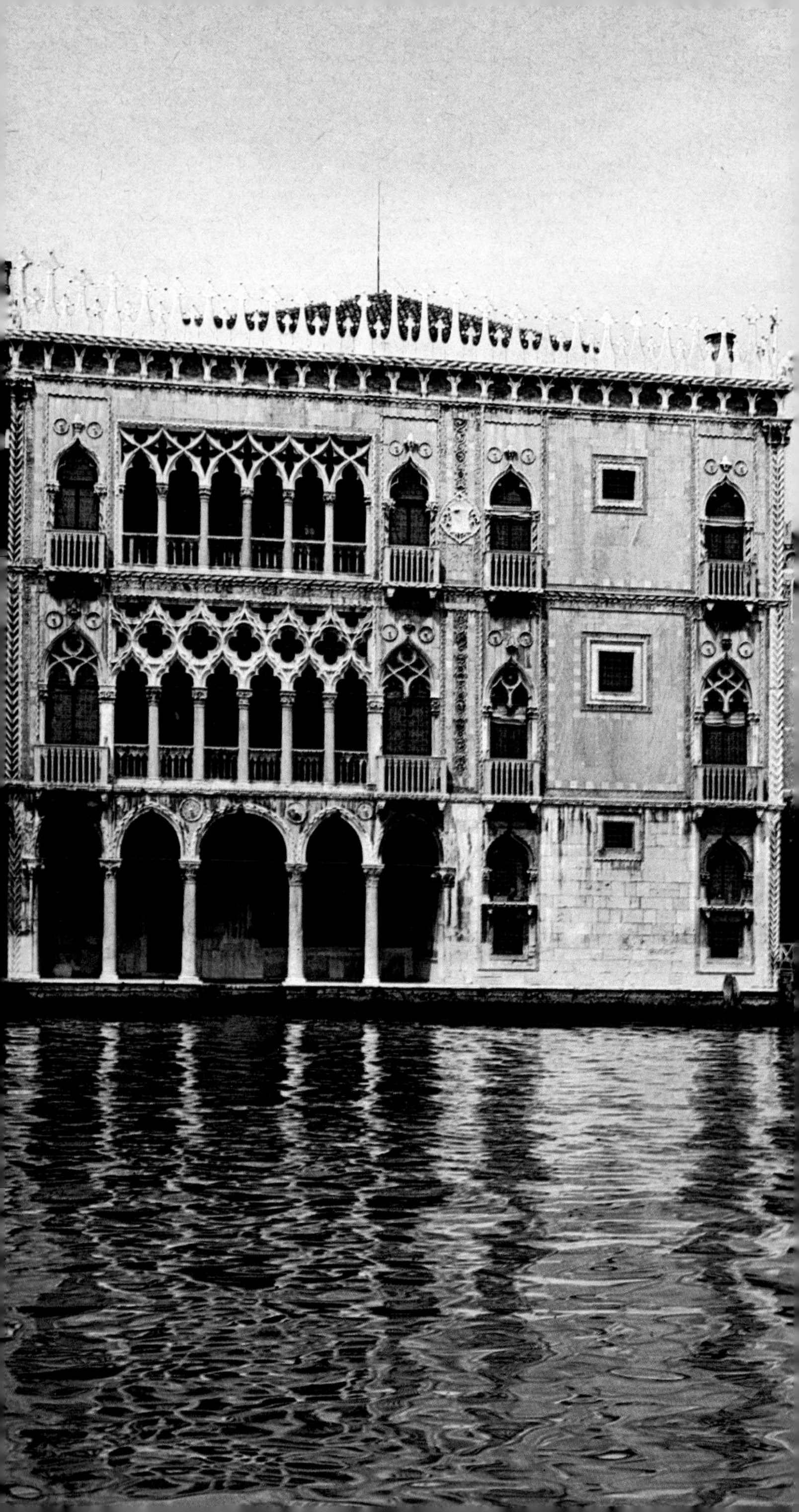

Ponte degli Scalzi.

CA' DA MOSTO - Venetian-byzantine style of the XIII century representing one of the most characteristic houses in Venice. Dwelling of the famous Mosta family of navigators.

PALAZZO MICHIEL DELLE COLONNE - of the XVII century and so called because of the pilasters of the portico.

Ca' d'oro.

New Buildings of Rialto.

PALAZZO SEGREDO - In gothic style of the end of the XIV century with a fine central window.

CA' D'ORO - The most beautiful palace on the Grand Canal, seat of the Franchetti Gallery (see description on page 136).

PALAZZO VENDRAMIN CALERGI - One of the most beautiful works in very elegant renaissance style. Begun by Coduccy, completed by Lombardo (1509). Richard Wagner died here on the 13th february 1883.

BRIDGE OF THE STATION OR OF THE SCALZI - Built in stone in 1934. It is the last of the three bridges that span the Canal.

The Warehouse of the Turks.

Old Buildings of Rialto.

FROM THE PONTILE SANTA CHIARA IN DIRECTION SAINT MARK, KEEPING ON THE RIGHT SIDE

FONDACO DEI TURCHI - Oriental type building with the facade in Venetian-byzantine style. It was entirely restored in 1869, following faithfully the original design and using the material obtained from the pre-existing building. Now seat of the Museum of Natural History.

PALAZZO PESARO - Imposing baroque building by Longhena. Seat of the Museum of Modern Art and the Oriental Museum (see description on page 143).

Ca' Pesaro.

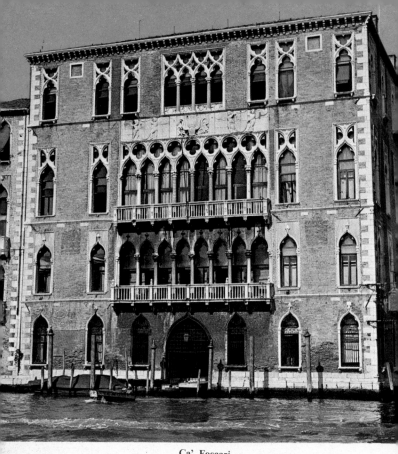

Ca' Foscari.

PALAZZO CORNER DELLA REGINA - classical building by Domenico Rossi (1724), it has been built on the pre-existing Palazzo dei Cornaro. It now houses the pawn-broking establishment.

FABBRICHE NUOVE DI RIALTO - An opera by Sansovino of poor forms, whose style is not much in tune with the other palaces on the Canal Grand. It is now the seat of the law courts.

PALAZZO DEI CAMERLENGHI - A renaissance Lombardian building by Guglielmo Bergamasco (1528).

PALAZZO DEI DIECI SAVI - Renaissance building from the beginning of the XVI century, an opera by Scarpagnino.

Ca' Rezzonico.

PALAZZO COCCINA-TIEPOLO-PAPADOPOLI - Beautiful classical construction of the XVI century, built by the architect Giacomo dei Grigi.

PALAZZO BERNARDO - Typical example of the gothic architecture with a facade that tunes well with the architectural and decorative lines. It was built in the XV century and sheltered the Duke of Milan Francesco Sforza.

PALAZZO PISANI - Another example of gothic architecture from the XV century. It is an imposing construction with a beautiful facade with rich decorative motives in the central-window.

PALAZZO BALBI - Called « in volta de Canal » because of its angular position. Work based on a design by Alessandro Vittoria (1590).

PALAZZO FOSCARI - Fine gothic building of the XV century with elegant decorations. It was erected

after the will of the Doge Foscari who led the Government of the Republic for over thirty years. It housed King Henry III from France.

PALAZZO REZZONICO - Imposing baroque palace, seat of the museum of the Settecento (see description on page 136).

PALAZZO LOREDAN - In gothic style of the XV century. The façade is very beautiful for its architectural and decorative motives. In the two lateral niches are two Lombardian sculptures of the XV century.

GALLERY OF THE ACADEMY - See description on page 120).

PALAZZO CONTARINI DAL ZAFFO - Renaissance, erected by Pietro Lombardo in the XV century, the façade is a typical example of Venetian-lombardian style.

The picturesque Church of St. Jeremy.

Church of Santa Maria della Salute.

PALAZZO DA MULE - Gothic building of the XV century.

PALAZZO DARIO - Renaissance, built in 1487 by Pietro Lombardo. Noteworthy are the graceful decorations of the multicoloured facade and the marble ornaments.

SANTA MARIA DELLA SALUTE - One of the most typical edifices of the Canal (see description on page 146).

PUNTA DELLA DOGANA - XVII century construction in tower form, surmounted by a sphere called « della fortuna ».

THE GALLERIES OF THE ACADEMY

HISTORY. We already know that in the Palace of the Port Authorities was founded in 1750 the Academy of painters and sculptors. It was later legally recognized during the presidency of Tiepolo and used to contain the experiments of the academicians. It was the contributions of these men, both in painting and sculpture, which constituted the first contribution to the formation of the Galleries. Here it seems fitting to explain why we say « Galleries » and not « Gallery of the Academy », since, we have seen, it is now a question of only one collection of paintings. When it was begun, however, the galleries were two; one was dedicated to paintings and the other to statues; or better still, to the gypsa taken from ancient sculptures of the Farsetti Collection and from the Canoviane. Once the gypsa had been taken to the Academy of Fine Arts, the name remained in the plural because the gallery was known in that way by everybody.

From Fonteghetto della Farina the Academy found in 1807 a more dignified home in the School and in the Church of Charity and in those of the ex-convent of the Canonici Lateranensi, a building by Palladio in 1560; In this headquarters were brought, besides the previously existing ones, many works originating from suppressed churches and convents. Thus, little by little from 1816 to 1856 it became rich with the Molin, Contarin, Renier, Manfrin Collections which contain most valuable masterpieces. Even the Italian State contributed to the increase of the collections through the interest of Directors Giulio Cantalamessa and Gino Fogolari.

A visit to the Galleries of the Academy is a real must for whomever goes to Venice; one can go as far as saying that it is impossible to appreciate the real essence of Venetian painting from the XIV to the XVIII centuries if we neglect this imposing, complex, graphic museum. Its intelligent arrangement, begun in 1945, gives the visitor the possibility of enjoying, under all conditions of space, light and visibility, the numerous pictorial works. Of these we shall cite, from one hall to another, the most significant and important ones.

HALL I. - This very beautiful place was the headquarters of the old Scuola Grande of Santa Maria della Carità (1400); we can enter it by means of a staircase built in 1765 adorned

Galleries of the Academy - BELLINI: Madonna degli Alberelli.

with two beautiful allegorical statues by Giammaria Morla-tier. The splendid fifteenth century ceiling is perhaps the work of Mario Cozzi; in the tondo is the « Eternal Father by Alvise Vivarini, in other tondos are figures of Prophets by Domenico Campagnola. The hall is dedicated to Venetian painters of the XIV century. The first work to be admired is the polyptych by Paolo Veneziano « Crowning of the Virgin » (and in the other compartments) « Stories of Christ and and Saint Francis ». Paolo is an artist who was formed in the Byzantine school, in his plainting we feel the reflection of mosaics in San Marco. Near him is Iacobello del Fiore's « Justice between Archangels Michael and Gabriel ». Let us note the beautiful impostation of Justice the forms and pictorial qualites of which remind us of the gracious style of Gentile da Fabriano. By Lorenzo Veneziano is the polyptych « Annunciation and Saints » and other paintings, of Byzantine formation which orients itself towards Gothic forms .To this contrasts Michele Giambono's polyptych « San Giacomo Maggiore among four Saints ». Let us also note the very beautiful painting which betrays some influence of Masolino da Panicale by Antonio Vivarini who has represented the « Wedding of S. Monica ».

HALL II. - Here are represented the great artists of the fifteenth century. First of all we note Giovanni Bellini's Madonna in throne and Saints » whose intensely aesthetic and mystic style manifests itself in all its beauty especially on account of the colour. Then we have Vittore Carpaccio with « Presentation of Jesus at the Temple » who reveals himself here as an academic painter. Then G.B. Cima with « Madonna in throne and Saints », a poetic, descriptive artists, full of candour. By him are also to be admired the « Madonna dell'Arancio » and « The incredulity of Saint Thomas ». Let us note the « Prayer in the Ochard » by Marco Basaiti who is the best of the minor artists. He feels the influence of Vivarini and is an effficient narrator.

HALL III. - First of all we should give a good look at the « Madonna and Child, Saint Catherine and the Baptist », a picture which was attributed to Giorgione at one time. Some essential differences with the latter, however, certainly make this the work of a pupil who has been very successful in interpreting the Romanesque idealism in opposition to the religious one. By Pordenone is an early work of his, « Madonna in throne » and by Basaiti is « Three Franciscan Saints ».

HALL IV. - Let us note immediately the great Piero della Francesca who is here present with « Saint Jerome and a faithful in a landscape »: his style is full of plastic and scientific realism which is translated into a geometric sense with wonderful luminous transparencies.

By Andrea Mantegan let us admire « Saint George » which expresses the power of conception of this great artists as well as his plastic and almost sculptorial energy. Another painter to be observed is Hans Memling who is here present with « Portrait of a Young Man », a painting which shows us how parallel were the relations between Flemish and Venetian arts. Let us not forget Cosmè Tura with his early work « Madonna and the Sleeping Child ». This artist felt the influence of the Paduan School and of Piero della Francesca, but distinguishes himself for his very relevant colouristic sense. Iacopo Bellini and his son Giovanni have two « Madonnas ». That of the former is still faithful to Gothic forms, that of the latter is decidedly detached from it. Always by Giovanni, but a Giovanni in his full maturity, let us note « Madonna between Saints Paul and George » and « Madonna between Saints Catherine and Magdalen ».

HALL V. - This hall is dominated by Giovanni Bellini and Giorgio Barbarelli called Giorgione. By the former let us note' his famous « Madonnas ». Let us look at the « Madonna degli Alberetti » and we shall become aware of the eminent qualities of the artist: smooth modelling, appropriate colouristic intonation, a reverent and mystic spirit, aerial luminosity: all requisites that make us love these valuable compositions of his.- By Giorgione is the much discussed and famous « Tempest ». This is a transition artist of the fifteenth and sixteenth centuries; in his paintings all is a dream, sweetness, melancholy;

Galleries of the Academy - MANTEGNA: **St. George,**

moreover he has a lyrical sense of the landscape and deals with the nude in a special colouristc way that announces the art of the great Titian. By him let us also see the expressive painting « The Old Lady », the work which has undergone an intelligent polish.

HALL VI. - A big textile which attracts our attention immediately is that of Paris Bordone; it represents « The Handing of the ring to the Doge » and refers to a miracle by Saint Marco who freed Venice from a terrible storm. The fisherman narrates the event to the Doge. This picture is one of the most famous ones in the Gallery not so much for the pictorial qualities of Bordone, but for the solemn framing af a particular architectural vision of Venice and for the bright colours of the great scene. Another notable artist is Bonifacio Pitati who is present with three works, but the most important one is certainly the « Parable of the Rich Epulon ». The scene is very beautiful, each character answers in full to his own attributes and is in perfect harmony with his surroundings. He also can be considered a precursor of Titian anl Iacopo Tintoretto. By the latter let us see the «Madonna of the Treausurers», he elaborates Michelangelo's style in his design and that of Titian in colour, he loves especially imposing and dramatic compositions which allow him to try more hardous and inexplored ways.

HALL VII. - By Lorenzo Lotto is a masterpiece: « Portrait of a Gentleman in His Studio ». This peculiar artist has refused to follow the artistic currents of his time and reaches here a narrative realism which characterizes his figures and, through light and colour, he knows how to give them that poetic touch which is by the way present in all his works. Almost the same requisites, even if to a smaller extent, we find in « S. Antonio Abate and S. Paul the Hermit » by Giovanni Girolamo Savoldo. These two figures full of sentiment and gravity, of precise designs of the fleeing light, seem immersed into hieratic shade which is appropriate to their life as hermits.

HALL VIII. - In this hall are parts of « The Sacred Conversation » by Iacopo Palma the Elder. The very beautiful painting shows us an artist who leaving the forms of Vivarini and of Bellini feels attracted to the art of Giorgione at first and of Titian later. Iacopo has pictorial qualities of neither artists; yet, here we note a certain freedom in representing nature as well as a vivacious colouring which put him quite near the great artist. By Gerolamo di Romano called Romanino let us observe the « Deposition ». He also reflects Giorgione and Tiziano's schemes, and possesses a rich and sumptuous colour, a Romantic temperament and an inventive capacity. Les us give a glance to the « Massacre of the Innocents » by Bonifacio de' Pitati and to the two works by Andrea Previtali « Christmas Scene » and « Christ on the Cross »: these works are quite interesting on account of the detailed manner of representing landscapes.

HALL IX. - In this hall are works by painters influenced by Tiziano. Bonifacio de' Pitati is well represented here with « Madonna between Saint Barbara and Saint Omobono » and the « Eternal Benedicante » and the picture « Tobiolo and Archangel Raphael » which was attributed to Tiziano as a young man. Critics, however, although recognizing very notable artistic qualities are inclined to attribute it to a follower on account of a certain compositive incoherence. By Tiziano, who tries his hand at imitating Michelanelo's style, is « Saint John the Baptist ».

HALL X. - Titian, Tintoretto and Paolo Veronese keep in this

Galleries of the Academy - CANALETTO: The Portico.

great hall their masterpieces. By Tiziano Vecellio, whose art is derived from Giorgione's, but who after knowing Michelangelo forms a style all his own which is an expression of power and effect and uses a rich and luminous colour, let us admire the « Pietà ». Much more represented, however, is his disciple Jacopo Robusti called Tintoretto. This artist loves great compositions and combines stylistic dictates of the Roman School with those of the Venetian School; from Michelangelo he acquires the strength of design; from Titian colour which he makes much use of in his intense and dramatic compositions.

To be convinced of this let us take a look at the four large cloths representing « The miracles of San Marco » and especially that of the « Saint who saves a slave from punishment », the « Carrying away of Saint Mark's Corpse », the « Dream of Saint Mark »; Also « Saint Mark saves a Saracen », the

Galleries of the Academy - GIORGIONE: **The Tempest.**

« Crucifixion », the « Presentation of Jesus to the Temple », the « Portrait of Solicitor Soranzo », the « Apparition of the Virgin to Saint Jerome ».

In the back of the hall a whole wall is occupied by the famous « Dinner-party at Levi's » by Paolo Veronese who originally intended to represent the « Last Supper of Jesus »; this work was judged irreverent by the Inquisition and the artist was compelled to change the title. Veronese derives his narrative art from Gentile Bellini and Carpaccio, influenced by Titian in his decorative sense.

Veronese's scenes are lacking in dramaticity, they are calm and festive, rich in architecture, and above all rich in chromatic refinements.

Galleries of the Academy - BELLINI: **Madonna and Child.**

Galleries of the Academy - BELLINI: **Pietà.**

Galleries of the Academy - PIAZZETTA: The Fortuneteller.

HALL XI. - This hall is divided into two sections; in the first are valuable paintings of the sixteenth century, in the second of the seventeenth and eighteenth. Let us once again meet Tintoretto with cloths representing « Saints » with the « Creation of Animals », Adam and Eve »; a beautiful group of works by Veronese among which the « Wedding of Saint Catharine », the Textiles « San Niccolò » received by the people of Mira », the « Stigmata of Saint Francis » and the very beautiful « Battle of Lepanto ». Among the works of the seventeenth and eighteenth centuries, let us note the « Party

Galleries of the Academy - Veronese: **Banquet in the house of Levi (detail).**

at the home of Simone di Bernardo Strozzi, the works of Pietro Berrettini da Cortona, of Luca Giordano, of Solimena. Above all are to be admired the works of the greatest Venetian eighteenth century painter: Giambattista Tiepola. If at the beginning the art of this artist has looked at pictorial tendencies of his contemporaries, when he meets Veronese, the impact is such that many pictorial qualities of Veronese become part of his art. Yet, Tiepola introduces a new elegance and subtlety which are typical of the eighteenth century. By him let us look at the imposing and luminous compositions « Saint Helen discovers the Cross », the « Frieze of the Bronze Snake », and the « figures of the faithful »: two vanes which were once par of the ceiling of the Church of Scalzi which was destroyed by a bomb in 1915 during the first world war.

HALL XII. - It is only a corridor in which are exposed a few Venetian landscape-painters. Here we note Marco Ricci, Giuseppe Zais and several works by Francesco Zuccarelli among which the « Rape of Europe ».

HALL XIII. - Here we return to the painting of the late sixteenth century. Worthy of attention are the works by Andrea Meldolla called Schiavone, especially the « Presentation of Jesus to the Temple »; by Iacopo da Ponte called Bassano is the very beautiful « Saint Jerome »; there are also a few portraits by Tintoretto among which « Doge Alvise Mocenigo » and « Attorney Andrea Cappelo ». By Jacopo Palma the Younger is the « Crucifixion of Saint Peter ».

HALL XIV. - We are here before painters of the seventeenth century among whom stands out the Roman Domenico Feti. Let us note the « Reading Girl », « Meditation » and « David » and « Isaac and Jacob ». Moreover we should observe the works by Govanni Liss, the « Sleeping Turk » by Pier Francesco Molá and « Jaint Jerome » by Bernardo Strozzi.

HALL XV. - This hall is made up of a corridor where are kept works of the eighteenth century. By Tiepolo is « Abraham and Angels », two allegories « Painting » and « Sculpture » by Giovanni Antonio Pellerini, an « Annunciation » by G.B. Pittoni and two gracious works by Giuseppe Bazzani.

HALL XVI. - Here are kept the early works of Tiepolo, the very beautiful « Fortune Teller » by Giovanni Battista Piazzetta, one of the most effective chiaroscuro workes in the Venetian School. In this work Piazzetta seems to favour scenes from Venetian life. Let us not forget to look at Longhi's « Painting and Merit » and « The Portrait of Carlo Lodoli »; by Vittore Ghislandi called Father Galgario. Let us admire also the very beautiful « Portrait of Count Vailati ».

HALL XVII. - In this hall which is shaped like a little gallery everything is to be admired. Here we meet famous landscape-painters and very pleasing Venetian scenes. Let us immediately look at one of the first landscape painters in Italy: Antonio Canal called Canaletto whose sharp narrative ability stems from fifteenth century art as represented by Bellini

Galleries of the Academy - CARPACCIO: **Stories of St. Ursula (detail).**

VICTOR CARPATHIVS
· M D X ·

and Carpaccio. Canaletto is present with « A view in perspective » made in 1765, however his most admirable Venetian scenes are in other Italian museums and at the Louvre.

Beside him we must note Francesco Guardi who, to Canaletto's coldness and objectivity, opposes an outstanding sense of shade as we can see in a « View of Saint George's island ». Let us note then the exquisite sketches of the « figurists » such as Sebastiano Ricci, Giambattista Pittoni, Piazzetta and Jacopo Amigoni. Even Tiepolo is present with a little sketch made for the ceiling of the Church of Scalzi.

Galleries of the Academy - CARPACCIO: **Arrival of the Ambassadors.**

Let us stop before the exquisite paintings of Pietro Longhi, « Dancing Lesson », the « Concert » the « Toilet ». We must look also at the pastels of Rosalba Carriera « Self-portrait » and the two portrait of « A French lady » and of a « Young man ».

HALL XVIII. - In this hall have been arranged eighteenth century paintings and sculptures. Among the paintings let us observe Tiepolo's earliest representing « Saint Joseph with Child and Saints ». By Canova (at the age of 18) is the group « The strugglers » and an « Apollo » in terracotta.

Galleries of the Academy - CARPACCIO: **Arrival of the Ambassadors (detail).**

HALL XIX. - Another corridor in which are also found fifteenth century works. Let us note the very beautiful « Christ at the column », perhaps by Pietro da Messina whose art is dominated by Antonello's influence; three works by Antonio Basaiti and other paintings belonging to minor artists dependent upon the schemes of the greatest teachers in the fifteenth century.

HALL XX. - This is the hall which contains works by Gentile Bellini the son of Jacopo. This painter was famous at his time, but has nothing to do with his father and with Giovanni Bellini. Gentile's art depends upon that of Mantegna; he loves huge compositions in which he recreates the sacred and profane magnificence of Venice in the fifteenth century. We can assert that all his work has the value of a historical document. To realize this let us look at the « Procession in San Marco Square » of 1496, the « Miracle of the relic fallen in the Canal of San Lorenzo ». Here we also find the the beautiful scene « Miraculous Healing of an Obsessed » by Vittore Carpaccio, also related to Gentile for his narrative historical sense, but who adds a lively imagination, as we can see in this work of great perspective and colouristic rigour.

Galleries of the Academy - CARPACCIO: **The Miracle of the Cross (detail).**

HALL XXI. - We reach this hall through a passage which allows us to see the noble architecture of Palladion in the internal facade of the ex convent of the Canonici Lateranensi. In the hall are exposed the great « teleri » of Vittore Carpaccio which represent episodes of the life of Saint Orsola. It is in these very «teleri» that all the art and fantasy of the painter are revealed; in them he reaches almost the ecstatic ideality of Beato Angelico. We can realize this by admiring the « Arrival of the Ambassadors », the « Departure of the Saint » and the « Sign of Saint Orsola ».

HALL XXII. - This hall is of neoclassical style of the first half of the ninenteenth century. We cross it returning from Hall XXI and we are let into a vast hall built out of the upper portion of the ex Church of Santa Maria della Carità.

HALL XXIII. - It is the above mentioned place in which we find again fifteenth century artists. The main works are the « Four triptych » by Giovanni Bellini, a few paintings with Saints by Carlo Crivelli, works by Alvise Vivarini, and the « Pietà » by Cima da Conegliano and the « Nude » by Giorgione.

HALL XXIV. - It has a beautiful carved and gilded ceiling. It is called Hotel of the School of Charity. The most important work here is Tiziano's « Mary as a Child presented at the Temple ». Let us note a very vast and imposing painting on cloth made in 1538 in which the artist reveals himself in all the power of his genius and of his pictorial experience. Let us admire the very beautiful architectures, the crowd of people, the woods and the mountains which are a nostalgic dream of Tiziano's native place Pieve di Cadore.

MUSEUM OF THE SETTECENTO

This is in the palazzo Rezzonico, that was the splendid dwelling of the Patriarchal family Rezzonico; it is of such richness that it represents the most splendid example of a noble residence of XVIII century Venice. The imposing Baroque construction is the work of Baldassare Longhena (1600) and finished by Giorgio Massari who added the third floor (1745). The English poet Robert Browing lived there in the XIX century. In 1935, the palace was acquired by the municipality of Venice, to form, in the sumptuous rooms, a collection of furniture and paintings of the XVIII century.

The first floor is reached by means of the main staircase, and from here one enters the ballroom with the magnificent inlaid forniture. There follows: Room of the Nuptial Allegory,painted by Tiepolo. Room of the Pastels, work of Rosalba Carriera. Room of the Tapestries, with Flemish tapestries. Throne Room, with the central fresco by Tiepolo and the former Nuptial Room, represents the finest room in the palace. Tiepolo Room, with allegorical frescoes of Fortune and Wisdom, and works by Alessandro Longhi. Room of the Library, with mythological subjects on the ceiling by Francesco Maffei. Lazzarini Room, containing his works. Room of Brustolon, with sculpture and rich forniture. Second Floor:. Portego, contains a collection of XVIII century works, amongst which: G. Battista Piazzetta, with *self portraits* and the *Death of Darius;* Giovanni Lys, with *Judith and Holofernes;* Giuseppe Zais, with landscapes; Francesco Zuccarelli and others. Room of Longhi. with a series of 34 small pictures of exquisite scenes from Venetian life and the frescoes of the ceiling by Tiepolo, with the *Triumph of Zephyr*. Room of the Parlatory, takes its name from the work of Guardi with the *Nuns' Parlatory*. One passes through a corridor into rooms exhibiting amusing scenes frescoed by Gian Domenico Tiepolo. On the third floor, apart from a series of painting and drawings by Longhi, Guardi and Tiepolo, the Room of the Costumes is interesting, where are exhibited the fashions of the time and the marionette theatre with a beautiful collection of marionettes, the best preserved of the time, and very dear to the Venetians.

FRANCHETTI GALLERY

This is in the palace called the Ca' d'Oro which takes its name from the gilding that once ornamented the facade that looks on to the Grand Canal. The building is the work of Bartolomeo Bon and Matteo Raverti (1421-40), commissioned by the procurator Marino Contarini. The palace, with its facade completely covered with polychrome marble, the portico on columns, the two areas with loggias and interwoven arches and the ancient battlements, presents the elaborate XV century Venetian

Ca' d'Oro - BORDONE: **Venus and Amor.**

Ca' d'Oro - ALLORI: **Allegory of the Wealth.**

style, and in the interior, the most magnificent example of a patrician dwelling of that time. The palace and the gallery were given to the state by Baron Giorgio Franchetti in 1916.

In the splendid courtyard with porticos and double flighted staircase, well ring by Bartolomeo Bon and on the walls, covered with marble, a Roman urn and Greek and Roman sculpture. On the first floor are numerous works amongst which of special importance are: *Annunciation* and *Joürney of the Virgin,* by Vittorio Carpaccio; The

Ca' d'Oro - VIVARINI: **Madonna and Child.**

Passion of Christ by Antonio Vivarini; *Venus with the Mirror,* by Titian; *St. Sebastian* by Mantegna. On the second floor, the most important works are: *Directors of the Mint* by Domenico Tintoretto; *Portrait of a Gentleman* by Van Dych; *Communion of St. Lucy* by G.B. Tiepolo; *Virgin with Child and two Angels,* by Filippino Lippi; *Saints,* by Domenico Ghirlandaio; *Flagellation,* by Luca Signorelli; *Piazzetta of St. Mark,* by Francesco Guardi; *Portrait of Nicolò Priuli,* by Tintoretto; *Portrait of a Girl,* by Pontormo, and also, a collection of medallions by Pisanello, Matteo de' Pasti, Sperandio and others. Amongst the sculpture, busts of Benedetto Manzini, by

Alessandro Vittoria; a Chinese bronze of the XV century, depicting the wanderer; bust of two youths, by T. Lombardo, and terracottas by Bernini and Maderno.

PAINTING GALLERY - QUERINI STAMPALIA

This is in the Querini palace (to the left of the church of St. Maria Formosa), seat of the public library. The gallery is on the second floor and in the 20 rooms of which it consists, besides a collection of forniture, porcelain, arms and musical instruments, it contains the works of Venetian painters from the XIV to the XVIII centuries.

In the first room, curious paintings with scenes from Venetian life, by Gabriele Bella. - Room II, *Coronation of the Virgin*, by Caterino and Donato Veneziano. - Room III, Portrait of Sebastiano Bombelli. - Room IV, works by Palma il Giovane, amongst which, *Adam and Eve* and *Self Portrait*. - Room V, Andrea Sciavone, with the *Conversion of St Paul* and other works. - Room VI-VII, works by the school of Venetian mannerists, amongst which, country scenes, by Matteo de' Pitocchi. - Room VIII-IX, works of the Renaissance, *Adoration of the Virgin*, by Lorenzo Credi; *Sacred Conversation*, by Palma il Vecchio; *Virgin with Child* and *Presentation in the Temple*, by Giovanni Bellini; Judith, by Vincenzo Catena. - Room XI-XII-XIII; works by Pietro Longhi with the *Seven Sacrament*, the *Hunt in the valley* and other works of the kind. - Room XIV, Marco, with various landscapes. - In Rooms XV to XX, collection of drawings by Giovanni Bellini, Titian, Raphael, Tintoretto, Veronese and others. Also, Flemish tapestries, furniture, arms, porcelain, laquered furniture in the Style of Louis XVI. - In room XVIII, *Portrait of G. Querini*, by G. Battista Tiepolo and in Room XX, *Virgin with Child*, by Bernardo Strozzi.

CORRER CIVIC MUSEUM

In the very new wing, or Procuratie Nuove in Saint Mark's Square has its headquarters the Correr Civic Museum. It was founded by Teodoro Correr, a distinguished personality of a Venetian patrician family, who donated to the Comune his magnificent collections in 1830. Here we only have one part of his collections: at the first floor is the Historical Museum, at the second is the Quadreria and the Renaissance Museum; while the eighteenth century museum is at Ca' Rezzonico and the Glass Museum of Murano at the No. 8 of the Fondamenta Giustiniane.

THE HISTORICAL SECTION. — We can enter the Historical Museum after reaching a hall in which we can admire the early masterpiece of the great sculptor Antonio Canova representing « Dedalus and Icar », the neoclassical decorations of the hall are by G. Borsato. The museum occupies thirty-three halls where are located the most varied souvenirs that give us a complete vision of the social life, of institutions, of art and history of the city. Here we can note: the Lion of Saint Mark, flags and symbols of the ancient Republic, portraits and coats-of-arms of the Doges, ducal bulls, descriptions of luxurious public ceremonies, objects belonging to dukes and high magistrates, souvenirs of the conspiracy of Bajamante Tiepolo, a splendid numismadic collection, documents and naval drawings the Battle of Lepanto, the Arsenal and the construction of ships, nautical papers and navigation instruments, great navigators and the great charter of colonial conquests, weapons, flags, coats-of-arms, canes of command, trofies.

THE QUADRERIA. — The very beautiful quadreria is contained in 19 halls. As it is impossible to list all the works, we shall indicate only the most important ones. The first one is dedicated to Venetian-byzantine painters; let us note the cover of the « trunk of Beata Giuliana » which perhaps goes back to the year 1200 and which presents Saints Biagio and Cataldo. In the second hall we have Venetian painters of the fourteenth century who got inspiration from the school of Paolo Veneziano. In the third hall: « Jesus Hands the Keys to Saint Peter » by Lorenzo Veneziano; in the fourth hall we can admire the very beautiful sculpture by Jacopo Dalle Masegne, it represents Doge Giovanni Mocenigo knealing. In the fifth hall are works the late-gothic Venetian painters; let us note the polyptich « Madonna Giving Milk » attributed to Guariento and by Stefano Veneziano « the Madonna and Child and Saint Christopher ». In the sixth hall continues the series of late-gothic Venetian painters, the most beautiful work is that of Jacobello del Fiore « Madonna and Child » and the « Madonna » by Giambono; in the seventh hall we note the splendid « Pietà » by Cosmé Tura, a masterpiece of high dramaticity of the great master of the Ferrarese school; in the eighth hall, together with other famous works by Ferrarese artists, we note particularly the two « Madonnas » by Bartolommeo Vivarini. In the ninth hall are interesting wooden sculptures; in the tenth hall is the Flemish painter Pietro Brueghel with a replica of « Adoration of the Magi », in the eleventh hall: the great Antonello da Messina is present with beautiful « Pietà » made about 1476.

In the twelvth hall are several works attributed to Flemish-german painters the exact attribution of them is uncertain; in the thirteenth hall are works by Bellini; let us note the « Crucifixion » by Iacopo or Giovanni Bellini, a portrait of Doge Giovanni Mocenigo by Gentile Bellini and a few works of Giambellini as a young man. In the fourteenth hall we see Alvise Vivarini's Saint Anthony from Padua », the other works are by painters who followed Vivarini and Giambellino; in the fifteenth hall is the very famous work « The Courtier Women » by the great Carpaccio; according to Ruskyn this is the « most beautiful painting in the world »; In the sixteenth hall we see, always by Carpaccio, the « Visitation » and « a Young Man Wearing a Red Cap »; by Pomezzano « Christ Carrying the Cross ». In the seventeenth hall is the « Crowned Virgin » and a « Virile Portrait » attributed to Lorenzo Lotto; eighteenth hall: dedicated to the « Madonneri » of the sixteenth century and of the seventeenth century; in the ninenteenth hall are gathered interesting sixteenth century ceramics among which are very beautiful for their artistic workmanship and fine execution those of the « Correr Service » which includes seventeen pieces the decoration of which is due to Niccolò Pellipario who made them about 1525. In the wall let us not the « Supper of San Domenico » a painting on cloth by Leandro Bassano.

THE RENAISSANCE MUSEUM. — It occupies about twenty halls in which are gathered souvenirs of the glorious struggle for the Renaissance. It was formed after the annexation of Venice to Italy in 1886 with a first gift by Piero Marsich, one of the protagonists of the defense of the city in the years 1848-49. Going through the halls we note: the fall of the Republic of Venice after a millennium of independence, the Napoleonic government, the Austrian dominion, the illustrated documentation of conspiracies, the liberation from the addition here are preserved flags, relics belonging to Austrians, the defense and fall of the city in 1849. In patriots, to Daniel Manin, weapons, paintings and water colours, documents and photographs referring to episodes of the national Renaissance. One hall is dedicated to the documentation of the Resistance to German occupation udring the second world war durin of the years 1943-45.

MODERN ART GALLERY

This is in the Pesaro palace, a baroque building, the most grandiose and elaborate on the Grand Canal, and work of Longhena (1710). The ground floor has large bosses and two floors have arcaded loggias. The gallery, founded in 1897, occupies the first two floors of the palace and contains many works by contemporary artists and is always being enriched by gifts, donations and purchases from the Biennale which takes place in Venice. On the third floor is The ORIENTAL MUSEUM, which has rich and precious material from the Far East, including sculptures, paintings, porcelain, ivory, and costumes from Japan, China, Java and other countries.

ARCHEOLOGICAL MUSEUM

This very important museum deserves its place in twenty rooms of the Procuratie Nuove. It was founded by Cardinal Domenico Grimani in 1523 and donated to the Republic; in it he collected marbles and bronzes found in Rome or from Greece, and it was enriched by important additions in 1586 by his nephew Giovanni Grimani, Patriarch of Aquileia. We will mention only the most important things in the various rooms: Room I - a rich collection of Greek and Roman epigraphy extremely interesting to the scholar; Room II - of interest to numismatists, for here in the four show-cases is an almost complete collection of Roman coins; Room III - beautiful examples of original Greek sculpture: No. 155 is « Erca-te », of the third century B.C., no. 262 is « Aphrodite Sosandra » from the fifth century B.C., No. 89 « Torso of Apollo »; Room IV - this is the room which contains works of rare beauty from the fifth and fourth centuries, all Greek originals. Notice No. 260, « Athena Acephala », No. 21 « Hera Grimani », in the centre « Persephone », from the Phidian epoch; Room V - Greek and Roman statues. Look at No. 126 « Ares and Aphrodite », no. 100 « Heracles and the ox ready for the sacrifice », No. 268 « Head of Athena »; Room VI - works created in the classic and Greek period. Worthy of note is No. 119, « Dionysius and a Satyr » and No. 263 is the famous « Ara Grimani » with scenes of Satyrs and Maenads; Room VII - No. 84 « Aphrodite Acephala », No. 67. « Funerary Stele of Lysandra, in a showcase the « Zulian Cameo » which came from Ephesus and represents Jupi-ter Egioco; Room VIII - Hellenic sculptures, the most important of which is No. 98 « Ulysses », a Roman copy of a Greek original from the third century B.C.; Room IX - beautiful collection of Roman portraits from the republican era in the third century A.D.; that of Pompey can be seen (No. 62) and in the centre of the room is No. 20, that of Vitellus; Room X - other Roman por-traits; Room XI - in the centre is a showcase with ivories and small bronzes, while around the walls are Greek and Roman reliefs; Room XII - here there are some beautiful sculptures, the majority representing the Goddess Venus, while in the centre No. 61 is « Aphrodite »; Room XIII - do not overlook the scene in relief of « Mitra sacrificing the bull » (No. 193); Room XIV - a lovely series of vases of exquisite work-manship; Room XV - an interesting collection of altars, reliefs and tablets from the Roman epoch; Room XVI - portraits of modern workmanship derived from archeo-logical models; Rooms XVII and XVIII - here are dis-played Egyptian sculptures and Greek reliefs belonging to the Correr Museum; notice No. 18 « Ares », and the Egyptian portraits Nos. 34 and 64; Room XIX - No. 13 is a beautiful sarcophagus of Roman artistry. and in the showcases are prehistoric objects, small bron-zes and Greek vases; Room XX - extremely interesting are the Egyptian mummies, and in the showcases are priceless Egyptian statuettes and Assyrian reliefs from the ninth and seventh centuries B.C.

Church of Santa Maria Gloriosa dei Frari.

THE MOST IMPORTANT CHURCHES OF VENICE

Santa Maria Gloriosa dei Frati. *(Campo dei Frari)* — This Franciscan church is one of the most important in Venice, and contains, like San Zanipolo, remains of great Venetians. Begun by the Franciscans in 1250, on a design attributed to Nicola Pisano, it was enlarged and modified by Scipione Bon in 1338, and completed in 1443. Romannesque-gothic in style, it has a tripartite facade with projecting pilasters with pinnacles. On the central doorway, statue by Alessandro Vittoria (1581). The Romanesque bell tower, after of Saint Mark's is the highest in Venice (1361-93).

The interior in the form of a Latin cross has three naves divided by 12 columns and is grandiose and simple in conformity, with the spirit of Franciscan churches. Besides the Mausoleum of Titian, it includes numerous monuments to illustrious Venetian personages from the XIV to the XVIII centuries. Right nave: first altar, of Longhena, statue by Giusto la Corte; second bay, tomb of Titian, who died in the plague of 1576 modest work of 1852, executed by pupils of Canova; third

145

altar, sculptures by Alessandro Vittoria amongst which is « Saint Jerome »; to the right of the right transept, monument to Jacopo Marcello, a Venetian admiral, work of Pietro Lombardo; on the following walls, monument to the Beato Pacifico, with the low relief depicting the « *Baptism of Christ* », by Nanni di Bartolo and Michael of Florence, XV century. In the sacristy, like an elegant little church, is preserved on the altar, a masterpiece of Giovanni Bellini: tripych in the original frame, with the « Virgin and Child Enthroned, musician angels and saints », (1488). In the third apse chapel to the right, triptych by Bartolomeo Vivarini; in the first chapel on the altar, « St. John the Baptist » by Donatello. Presbytery: right wall, monument to the Doge, Francesco Foscari, Renaissance-gothic, by the brothers Bregno (1457, apprat.); in the left wall monument to the Doge Nicolò Tron, a Renaissance jewel by Antonio Rizzo. 1476; behind the high altar, the famous altarpiece of the « Assumption », by Titian, one of the greatest compositions of all time, imitated by many artists, even famous ones, without success (1518). In the first apse chapel to the left, beautiful altarpiece by Bernardo Licinio (1535); in the third chapel, on the altar, altarpiece with « Saint Ambrose enthroned », by Alvise Vivarini and Marco Basaiti (1503); in the fourth chapel, on the altar triptych, by Bartolomeo Vivarini and on the baptismal font, statue of Saint John the Baptist, by Jacopo Sansovino (1554), Left nave: on the second altar, altarpiece with the « Virgin of the Pesaro family » masterpiece by Titian (1526); further along, large monument to Doge Giovanni Pesaro, by Longhena (1669); there follows the mausoleum of Antonio Canova, constructed on designs of the master himself.

Santa Maria della Salute. *(Campo Salute)* — The construction of the church was ordered on the 22nd of October 1630, by the Senate, to thank the Virgin at the end of the terribile plague that had claimed about 47,000 victims. The task was given to Baldassare Longhena (1631-87) who created that masterpiece of Venetian-baroque architecture which can be admired. It has an octagonal plan surmounted by a dome with the great facade facing the Grand Canal.
The simple and grandiose interior is also octagonal, with arcades on which is placed the tamburo of the cupola, and six lateral chapels. In the first altars to the right,

Church of Santa Maria Gloriosa dei Frari - TITIAN: Assumption.

paintings by Luca Giordano, with the « Presentation of Mary Assumption » and « Nativity of Mary »; in the first altar on the left, « Pentecost », late work by Titian. The marble group on the high altar depicting the « Plague fleeing before the Virgin », is the work of Giusto la Corte. In the large sacristy, stupendous works by Titian; in the ceiling, « Death of Abel, Sacrifice of Abraham, David and Goliath » (1543), and on the altar, « St. Mark and Saints », youthful work of 1512. On the walls, diverse works by various artists among which, The « Wedding in Canaan », one of the masterpieces of Tintoretto.

San Zaccaria. — (*Campo S. Zaccaria*). It is one of the most characteristic churches in Venice, erected in the IX century and transformed between the XV and XVI centuries by Antonio Gambello and Mauro Caducci, who gave to the facade with six orders all its splendour creating one of the most marvelous works of Venetian Renaissance. Above the doorway, Saint Zachariah, a statue by Alessandro Vittoria.

The interior has three naves divided by high columns, with Gothic apse and chapels radiating from the external wall. Along the walls large canvases by the most important painters of the XVII century. On the second altar on the left, the celebrated altarpiece with the « Virgin and Child and Saints », masterpiece by Giovanni Bellini (1505). From the right nave, one enters the chapel of St. Athanasius, with beautiful Gothic stalls (1544-64) and the « Virgin and Saints » by Palma il Vecchio and above the door, « Birth of St. John the Baptist », by Tintoretto; from here one enters the chapel of Saint Tarasio, which is the jewel of the church with the apse of the old original temple in which have come to light important frescoes by the Florentine Andrea del Castagno, with the « Eternal Father and Saints » (1442); on the walls three wooden ancons, with two magnificent polyptyches by Giovanni Alemagna and Antonio Vivarini. At the end of the left nave, the sepulchre with a bust self - portrait, by Alessandro Vittoria, buried here (1605) and now left in this church, and two holy water stoups, works of exquisite craftsmanship.

Campo San Zanipolo and Church of San Giovanni e Paolo. The equestrian statue of the condottiere Bartolomeo Colleoni which stands in the middle of this square, is by Andrea del Verrocchio.

Campo di San Zanipolo. — This is the most picturesque piazza in the city, after Piazza San Marco. It contains the facades of the church of St. John and Paul and the School of St. Mark with the annexed church of St. Lazarus of the Beggars. In the centre stands the equestrian statue

of the famous Bergamo condottiere Colleoni, the Renaissance masterpiece of the Florentine Andrea del Verrocchio
(1488); who was the master of Leonardo da Vinci. When
the master died, his work was finished by the Venetian
Alessandro Leopardi, who created the elegant pedestal

Saint Giovanni and Paolo or Saint Zanipolo. — Begun by the Dominicans in 1246, it was finished in 1430. Grandiose church, constituting, like that of the Franciscans of the Frari, a notable example of religious Gothic-Venetian architecture. In the interior are the remains of the famous Venetian who had merited the recognition of the Serenissima. On the facade, incomplete, there are Byzantine sculptures and in the rich marble doorway, by Bartolomeo Bon, elementes of Gothic and Renaissance characters are mingled. The interior is in the form of a Latin cross with three naves divided by ten columns, with central apse and four lateral ones. In the walls of the entrance, three Mocenigo monuments, of which of great importance is that of Doge Pietro Mocenigo, by Pietro Lombardi (1485), to the right. On the first altar of the nave, « Virgin and Saints », by Francesco Bissolo; second altar, polyp of « San Vincenzo Ferreri » by Giovanni Bellini, 1465; afterwards the chapel of the Addolorata, from which one enters the Baptistry; on the walls, monuments of the family of the Doges Valier, work planned by Andrea Tiraldi (1700); at the end of the nave, chapel of St. Dominic, elaborately decorated and with the vault of the ceiling frescoed by Piazzetta, with the Glory of St. Dominic, one of the finest works of the artist, 1727. In the right transept, « Christ below the Cross », by Alviese Vivarini; « St. Anthony and the Poor » by Lorenzo Lotto (1542), and on the second altar, « Christ and Saints » by Rocco Marconi. Magnificent Gothic window, by Bartolomeo Vivarini, XV century. Presbytery: of imposing appearence with the polygonal luminous apse and the Baroque high altar, it has on the right, the XIV century monument to Doge Michele Marosini, with the mosaic of the Crucifixon in the lunette and further on, the monument to Doge Leonardo Loredan (1572); to the left, monument to Doge Andrea Vendramin, by Pietro and Tullio Lombardo, XV century, and the monument to Doge Marco Corner, with statue of the Virgin by Nino Pisano. At the end to three left transept, monument to Doge Antonio Vernier, by the Dalle Masegne and below, the entrance door to the XVI century chapel of the Rosario, that once contained works of sculpture by Alessandro Vittoria and paintings by Tintorretto,

Equestrian statue of Bartolomeo Colleoni.

Bassanò and others, but, unfortunately, these works were destroyed in the fire of 1867; in the reconstucted ceiling, there are three works by Veronese, with the « Annunciation », «Assumption» and «Adoration of the Shepherds»; on the walls. Statues by artists of XVIII century and two bronze candelabras by Alessandro Vittoria. From the left nave, one enters the luxurious sacristy, with canvases by Palma the Younger. Under the organ, remains of a triptych by Bartolomeo Vivarini. Futher on, monument to Doge Pasquale Malipiero, by Pietro Lombardo; there follows the monument to Senator Bonzi and one to Doge Tomaso Mocenigo, work of Tuscan artists of the XV century, and that of Doge Nicolò Marcello by Pietro Lombardo and on the first altar, statue of Saint Jerome, by Alessandro Vittoria.

Madonna dell'Orto. — *(Fondego Madonna dell'orto).* Originally dedicated to St. Christopher, it was constucted at the end of the XIV century, and has a facade which is Romanesque in the arrangement of the masses and Gothic in its decoration. The statues of the apostles, in the niches of the slanting galleries, are by the school of the Dalle Masegne. The basilical interior has three naves divided by ten marble columns and a polygonal apse. It contains numerous paintings by Iacopo Robusti, called Tintoretto, who was buried here (1594) and his tomb decorated with an extremely simple stone is in the chapel to the right of the Presbytery. On the first altar of the right nave, « St John the Baptist in Ecstasy and Saints », masterpiece by Cima da Conegliano (1943); above the chapel of St. Mauro, « Presentation of Mary in the Temple », by Tintoretto. The large canvases in the Presbytery, with the « Last Judgement », the « Worship of the Golden Calf » and « Moses receiving the tables of the Law », are works by Tintoretto, who painted them in his full creative maturity (1546); by him also in the fourth chapel of the left nave is the masterpiece with « St Agnes raising Licinio from the dead ». In the first chapel, « Virgin and Child » by Giovanni Bellini.

Sant'Alvise. — *(Campo S. Alvise).* XIV century church of Gothic architecture, in the interior of which are three wonderful canvases by Tiepolo: two on the right wall with the «Crowning with Thorns» and the «Flagellation» and to the right of the main chapel, the « Journey to

Calvary ». Under the choir, a series of 8 small panels by a painter of the XV century, which John Ruskin attributed to the young Carpaccio.

Sant'Aponal. — (*Sestiere di San Polo*). This is the church of St. Apollinare, the facade of which dates back to 1400. The Crucifixion and scenes from the Life of Christ on the portal were done in 1294.

The building was begun in the eleventh century in the Gothic style. There is one aisle only, and the altars are Renaissance. On the high altar is the « Martyrdom of St. Apollinare » by L. Querena, and on the other altars are paintings of the eighteenth and nineteenth centuries. The statues are varied in period and origin. The beautiful campanile (bell-tower) is in Romanesque style, with Gothic additions. Under the portico is one of the most ancient emblems of the Republic: the lion of St. Mark with a closed book, in bas-relief, from the thirteenth century.

SS. Apostoli. — (*Sestiere di Cannaregio*). The original church was very ancient, but it has been rebuilt several times, and underwent a radical renovation in 1575. In the field where it stands, notice how along one side of the church there is a civilian house which has been built between the campanile and the cupola of the Corner Chapel. The campanile was built in 1672, and the belfry was added by Andrea Tirali. The facade is of brick, and is of no particular interest. The rectangular interior consists of one aisle. On the ceiling is « Exaltation of the Eucharist » and « The Apostles », frescoes of masterful composition by Fabio Canal and G. Gaspari (1748). The Corner Chapel is on the right; it was not reconstructed in the sixteenth century and the Lombardesque style of architecture is attributed to Mauro Coducci. On the right-hand wall is the « Tomb of Marco Corner » attributed to Tullio Lombardo, and on the left is that of the Cardinal Giorgio Corner. On the altar is the lovely altar-piece of the « Communion of St. Lucia » by Giovan Battista Tiepolo, and in the following one is the « Birth of the Virgin » by G. Contarini. In another chapel to the right of the main chapel can be seen the remains of frescoes in the byzantine style describing the episodes « Deposition from the Cross » and « The Burial of Christ ». A short distance away is a bas-relief by Tullio Lombardo (sixteenth century) of « St. Sebastian ». In the Presbytery to the right is the « Last Supper » by Cesare da Conegliano (sixteenth century) and to the left is the « Falling of manna », school of Paolo Veronese.

The Carmini. — *(Sestiere di Dorsoduro e Giudeer).* Church erected in the XIV century in Romanesque-Gothic style and restored in the XVII century. The Renaissance facade has a very beautiful « porch » of the original construction in the left side. The interior has three naves divided by 24 Romanesque columns. On the second altar of the right naves; « Adoration of the Shepherds and Saints » by Cima da Conegliano (1510); in the chapel to the right of the Presbytery the « Deposition », a low bronze relief by the school of Donatello and perhaps by Verrocchio; on the second altar of the left nave, « Saints Nicolò, Battista, and Lucia » with a beautiful landscape by Lorenzo Lotto. The adjacent cloister is intersting.

San Cassiano. — *(Sestiere di S. Polo).* This church dates back to the tenth century, but was rebuilt in the seventheenth century. The towers is constructed of great square blocks, the belfry with fine columns in Gothic style is a fifteenth century addition. The lovely interior consists of three tall aisles, with a cross vaulted ceiling. On the ceiling are frescoes by Cedini, while those in the lunettes are by G.D. Tiepolo. The paintings above the parapet of the organ: « Stories of San Cassiano » were painted by arstis of the school of Veronese. The high altar is the work of A. Meyrin (1684). Iacopo Tintoretto painted the altar-piece « Resurrection and two Saints » as well as the paintings on each side: « Descent into the Limbo » and « Crucifixion »; the first was done in 1584, and the paintings in 1568. After the Sacristy notice the Chapel of St. Charles, decorated in the eighteenth century with beautiful marquetry in marble; on the ceiling is « San Cassiano and St. Catherine » by G. Batt. Pittoni, who also painted the « Madonna in Glory with Saints » on the altar, while on the walls are « The Martyrdom of St. Cassiano » by A. Balestra, and « The Sermon in the Orchard » by Leandro Bassano.

San Francesco della Vigna. — *(Campo Confraternita).* Sixteenth century church, constructed by Jacopo Sansovino, while the facade, grandiose and harmonious adorned

Cannaregio Canal.

with two bronze statues, is by Palladio. The vast
interior in the form of a Latin cross with one nave, is
rich in works of art. On the first altar of the right transept,
rare canvas by Antonio da Negroponte, painter of the XV
century, rich in fantasy and sweet harmony, the « Virgin
enthroned in adoration »; in the chapel the left of the
Presbytery, an interesting cyclede of sculptures by Pietro
Lombardo and pupils; from left transept one enters
the Holy chapel, which contains a « Virgin and Saints »,
by Giovanni Bellini (1507); in the sacristy, triptych by
Antonio Vivarini, with « Saint Jerome, Saint Bernard »
and « Saint Lodovico »; in the fifth chapel to the left,
« Holy Conversation », by Veronese (1551).

Chiesa di Gesuati.— (*Sestiere di Dorsoduro*). This church is also known as S. Maria del Rosario, and was constructed in 1726-43 for the Dominicans by the architect Giorgio Massari. It stands in the land of a fourteenth century convent known as that of the « poor Jesuits ». The facade is of the classic order, and the single aisle in the beautiful interior is elliptical in form, with a presbytery with a cupola, and side chapels. On the ceilingare G.B. Tiepolo's frescos « The Glory of St. Dominic, the Institution of the Rosary, St. Dominic and the Madonna, and the Mysteries of the Rosary ». Beginning the visit with the altars to the right: the first altar — a masterpiece by Tiepolo « Madonna in glory with three saints (1747); second altar — « St. Dominic » by G.B. Piazzetta, who also painted the third altar « S. Vincenzo Ferre, Giacinto and Lodovico Bertrando (1739). In the presbytery the cupola frescoes were done by Tiepolo; there is a precious high altar, and a choir of the eighteenth century. On the wall is « The Virgin and St. Anne » by M. Ingoli. On the left-hand side of the third altar is a « Crucifixion » by Jacopo Tintoretto, on the first altar the « Saints Pius V, Thomas of Aquinas and Peter Martyr » by Sebastiano Ricci, and on the altar the « Madonna and child » is attributed to Stefano Plebano.

Chiesa dei Gesuiti. — (*Sestiere di Cannareggio*). This grandiose church which was founded in the twelfth century for the Crucifers, passed in 1656 to the Jesuits, and was rebuilt by Domenico Rossi in 1715-30. The imposing facade is in the baroque style, by the architect G. Batt. Fattoretto, with statues of the twelve Apostles by F. Penso, the brothers Groppelli and P. Baratta. On the portal the angels are by Matteo Calderoni, on the tympanum « Assumption » by G. Torretto. The interior is in the form of a Latin cross, with a striking decoration of multi-coloured marble tarquetry. The stucco ceiling is by A. Stazio, and the frescoes by Fontebasso. In the entrance wall is a monument of G.B. Longhena, and a bust of Priamo da Lezze, the work of Jacopo Sansovino.

In the first altar on the right is the « Guardian Angel » by Palma il Giovane; in the second is a statue of « St. Barbara » by Morlaiter; in the third is a « Madonna and Saints » by Balestra; in the transept on the right of the altar is a statue of « St. Ignatius » by P. Baratta;

in the chapel on the right beside the main chapel is « The Preaching of S. Francesco Saverio » by P. Liberi. In the presbytery the rich architecture inspired by Bernini is by Padre G. Pozzo, the sculptures by Torretto and the frescoes by L. Dorignay. Notice the « Assumption » by Jacopo Tintoretto and the « Martyrdom of St. Lawrence » by Titian. In the Sacristy is a pictorial cycle with episodes of the Order of the Crucifers, by Palma il Giovane, done in 1589-93.

San Giacomo dall'Orio. — (*Campo S. Giacomo*). Of very ancient origin, it was altered during the Renaissance and restored in 1909. The XIII century bell tower is Romanesque with graceful double lighted windows. The interior is in the form of a Latin cross with three naves, with wooden ceiling. The new sacristy, with access from the right transept, has a ceiling painted by Verones with « Allegories of the Faith » and on the walls, paintings of the same, by Francesco Bassano and Giovanni Buonconsiglio called Marescalco (1511). In the Presbytery, « Virgin with Child and Saints », by Lorenzo Lotto. Through the door on the left of the main chapel, one enters the old sacristy, with the walls adroned with canvases by Palma the Younger (1575).

San Giobbe. — (*Campo S. Giobbe*). Lombardesque construction, it was begun in 1451. The elegant doorway is by Pietro Lombardo and the beautiful bell tower is Romanesque-Gothic. The interior has one nave with altars to the right and chapels to the left. The Presbytery and the two small chapels that flank it, is an admirable Renaissance work by Pietro Lombardo, while the beautiful tomb stones of Doge Cristopher Moro and his wife Cristiana Sanudu, in the floor, are the work of his pupils. In the second chapel to the left, work of Tuscan artists of the XV century, in the vault, medallions in terracotta by the Della Robbia, and on the sacristy is a triptych by Antonio Vivarini.

San Giovanni in Bragora. — (*Sestiere di Castello*). It appears to have been founded in the eighth century, but was reconstructed in 1475. The unusual name is probably from the Greek work « agorà » (square) or from the dialectal « bràgola » (square in the market). The

Island of San Giorgio Maggiore and the church of the same name by Palladio and Scamozzi. It was begun and finished between 1565 and 1610. In the interior, masterpieces by Michelozzi, Tintoretto and Carpaccio.

beautiful facade is of late Gothic Venetian style, and the Gothic interior consists of three aisles, and a truss roof. Above the entrance is « Christ before Caifa » by Palma il Giovane, while on the walls of the nave and on the triumphal arch are « The Annunciation, Saints », and other frescoes of popular character by Tommaso di Zorzi, in the fifteenth century; in the second chapel of the right aisle is an altar-piece with « St. John the almoner » and in the lunette is « The Transferring of the

Body of the Saint to Venice » by Iacopo Marieschi, and under the altar is the urn with the body of the Saint. On the door of the sacristy which is at the end of the aisle, notice the « Christ blessing » by Alvise Vivarini (1493). The presbytery in Renaissance style is by the architect Sebastiano Mariani (1485-88); the entrance pilasters are, to the right, « St. Helen and Constantine at the sides of the Cross », and to the left: « Christ risen », both of which are the work of Viva-

163

rini. On the main altar are three statues: « Faith », « St. John the Evangelist » and « St. John the almoner »; the first is by Antonio Gai, the second by Morlaiter, the third by Giovanni Marchiori. Now move on to the apse, to see « The Baptism of Christ » by Cima da Conegliano. On the walls are « The Last Supper » by Paris Bordone and « The Washing of the feet », by Palma il Giovane. In the left aisle is the entrance to the chapel beside the presbytery, where on the right is a triptych with predella by Bartolomeo Vivarini: « Madonna between St. Andrew and John the Baptist », and on the left is Francesco Bissolo's « Saints Andrew, Jerome and Martin ».

San Giovanni Crisostomo. — (*Sestiere di Cannaregio*). This church was founded in 1080, but its location was on the Grand Canal, and it was destroyed by a fire in 1475, and reconstructed here by Mauro Coducci (1497-1504). The facade is crowned by simple curves, beside the beautiful sixteenth century campanile.

The interior is in the form of a Greek cross, with a barrel vault and a central cupola. Above the first altar on the right is « Saints Christopher, Jerome and Augustine » by Giovanni Bellini, a masterpiece executed by the great artist in his old age (1513). Beside the altar are « Saints John Chrysostom, Onofrio, Andrew and Agatha » by Giovanni Mansueti which at one time formed the doors of the old organ. On the main altar is the celebrated altar-piece by Sebastiano del Piombo « St. Chrysostom and five Saints », which was done in 1509.

San Giovanni Elemosinario. — (*Sestiere di San Polo*). Dates back to 1071, but was destroyed by a fire in 1513 and reconstructed in 1530 by Scarpagnino. However the lovely campanile is the original (1398-1410) as it was saved from the fire. The interior is on a Greek cross with a cupola. On the entrance wall is L. Corona's « Crucifixion » and his « Falling of manna » is on the right-hand wall; in the chapel to the right of the high altar there is a beautiful painting by Pordenone: « Saints Sebastian, Catherine and Rocco ». In the Sacristy G.B. Pittoni has painted in the ceilling « St. Augustine » and on the altar « Madonna and St. Philip ». In the presbytery, on the main altar is a masterpiece by Titian (1545) « St. John the almoner »; in the lunette is a « Resurrection » by L. Corona, and

on the walls are two other works by the same artist
« The Sermon in the Orchard » and « Crucifixion »
while on the left the « Last Supper » is by Aliense.
On the left-hand wall of the church is « Constantine
with the Cross » by Palma di Giovane, and on the
door on one side are three panels by Marco Vecellico:
« St. John the almoner », « Visit of the Doge Donato
to the church » and « St. Mark ».

San Giorgio Maggiore. *(Isola di S. Giorgio)* — The basilica is one of the finest works by Palladio (1565-80')
which was finished, according to his drawings, by
Scamozzi (1610). The facade which revals once again
the personal style of Palladio, is divided into three
spaces by four columns with Corinthian capitals. In the
two niches, between the columms, the statues of Saint
George and Saint Stephen and in the wings the bust
of Doges Tribuno Memmo and P. Ziani, by Giulio dal
Moro. The bell tower is from 1791 and is the work of
Benedetti Buratti, in replacement of that which collapsed in 1773; from the top one enjoys a very beautiful
panorama of Venice and of the lagoon.
The simple and grandiose interior is in the form of an
inverted Latin cross, with three naves and cupola. On
the second altar to the right, wooden « Crucifix », by
Michelozzo, a Florentine. In the Presbytery, on the high
altar, beautiful bronze group, by Girolamo Campagna
(1593) and on the walls, two masterpieces by Tintoretto:
to the right, « Last Supper » and on the left, « Fall of
the Manna »; in the apse, magnificent inlaid wood choir,
of 1598. In the annex monastery, on can visit the Chap-
ter house, where on the 12th of March 1800 Pius II was
elected Pope, and on the altar one can admire « Saint
George killing the Dragon », work of Carpaccio and
the chapel of the Dead, with the « Deposition », admirable work by Tintoretto.

San Giuliano. — *(Sestiere di San Marco)*. A tradition
says that this church was founded in '829, but it was
rebuilt in 1553 by Iacopo Sansovino assisted by A. Vittoria, financed by Tommaso Rangone, doctor and philo-
logist from Ravenna, whose statue in bronze, the work
of Sansovino, is placed on the portal, flanked by symbols
of the Sciences. The interior is square, with a single
aisle, and in the richly engraved ceiling is « Glory of

Church of Santa Maria Formosa. Its origin goes back to the seventh century. Rebuilt by the architect Codussi in 1492, it has two façades. One overlooking a canal, and the other facing the Campo Santa Maria Formosa.

St. Julian » by Palma il Giovane with « Virtue and Prophets » by L. Corona. Over the first altar to the right is « St. Rocco » by S. Peranda, « St. Mark and Jerome » by L. Bassano, and high up is a « Pietà » by Paolo Veronese (1584); on the second altar is « The Assumption » by Palma il Giovane. In the presbytery on the altar is « The Coronation of the Virgin and Saints » by G. Santacroce, on the walls are « The Miracle of St. Julian » and « The Martyrdom of the Saint »

by A. Zanchi. To the left is the Chapel of the Sacrament
by the architect G.A. Rusconi, with a stucco ceiling by
A. Vittoria; on the altar is an high-relief in marble
depicts the « Pietà » work, and there are statues in
terracotta of « Madonna » and « Magdalene » by G.
Campagna. On the second altar to the left is « Sacred
Heart and Saints » by Guarana, and on the first is
« Madonna enthroned and Saints » by Boccaccio Boc-
caccini.

Santa Maria del Giglio. — (*Sestiere di S. Marco*). Is also known as Santa Maria Zobenigo because it was founded by the Iubanico family, apparently in the ninth century. It was restored in 1680-83, through the munificence of the Barbaro family, by Giuseppe Sardi. It has a lovely baroque facade with the statues of the two founders and planimetrical views of the cities of Zara, Candia, Padua, Rome, Corfù and Spalato. The interior consists of one rectangular aisle, ceiling with paintings by A. Zanchi. An interesting chapel to the right is the Molin Chapel, in the ceiling of which is a « Madonna » attributed to Domenico Tintoretto. On the walls notice the painting « The Ascent to Calvary » perhaps by Fontebasso; on the second altar is a statues of Beato Gregorio Barbarigo by Morlaiter, on the third is « The Visitation » by Palma il Giovane. In the seventeenth-century sacristy is « Madonna and child and young St. John » by P. Rubens. In the presbytery is the « Monument of Marco Giulio Contarini » by Vittoria, and on the main altar are statues by E. Meyring of « Gabriel » and « The Virgin Mary ». In the third altar to the left is « Christ and the Saints Justina and Francesco da Paola » by Iacopo Tintoretto.

Santa Maria Mater Domini. — (*Sestiere di Santa Croce*). Is a beautiful church in Renaissance style with a harmonious facade attributed to Sansovino, and the interior consists of three aisles. To the right, on the first altar, are « Statues of Saints Peter and Paul » by Lorenzo Bregno (1524), in the second is « St. Christine » by Vincenzo Catena. In the transept is a « Last Supper » by Pitati, behind the high altar in the central apse is a beautiful « Madonna and Child » a Tuscan stucco from the fifteenth century. In the left-hand apse is a fifteenth century altar with « Statues of St. Mark and St. John » by Bregno. In the left transept is a very beautiful composition in « chiaroscuro » by Iacopo Tintoretto « Invention of the Cross ». In the Sacristy is a tapestry-banner carried out by A. Dini to a design by G.B. Tiepolo « Madonna and Child ».

Santa Maria Formosa. — (*Calle delle Baude*). Very ancient in origin, it was rebuilt in 1492 by Mauro Coducci. It has two XVI century facades and a baroque bell

Rio San Moisé.

tower of the XVII century. The interior, in the form of a Latin cross, has only one nave. In the first chapel to the right, a beautiful triptych by Bartolomeo Vivarini, with the « Nativity of Mary, the Virgin of the Misericord », transcept, « St. Barbara and Four Saints », celebrated polyptich by Palma the Elder, 1509.

Santa Maria dei Miracoli. — (*Sestieve di Cannareggio*). Renaissance church constructed by Pietro Lombardo in 1481. It has an original and elegant facade with marble ornaments on the two floors with central door, surmounted by two large windows. The rectangular has its walls covered with precious marble and the barrel-vaulted ceiling is decorated with 50 panels of the heads of pro-

Church of
San Moisé
dating from
the eighth
century.
It was
reconstructed
in the tenth
century by
Moisé Venier
who gave it
the name of
his saint.
The façade,
in a baroque
style, is by
Tremignon and
A. Meyering
(1668).

Partial view of Campo San Polo.

phets and saints, by Piero Pennacchi, 1528. The raised Presbytery has an elegant stairway and the high altar is covered by a cupola; the whole, by the brothers Lombardo, is a prodigious wonder of decorative art.

San Moisè. — (*Sestiere di San Marco*). This church dates back to the eighth century, but has been rebuilt several times. The campanile was built in the fourteenth century, while the splendid baroque facade was added by A. Tremignon in 1668. The seventeenth century interior consists of one aisle, and on the ceiling is « The Vision of Moses », perhaps by Niccolò Bambini. It is rich in marbles and paintings of the seventeenth and eighteenth centuries. In the Sacristy is a remarkable bas-relief in bronze: « Deposition » by Niccolò and Sebastiano Roccatagliata. In the presbytery is a baroque sculpture designed by Tremignon and executed by E. Meyring, representing « Mount Sinai with Moses receiving the tablets of the laws ». In the chapel to the left is « The Washing of the feet » by Iacopo Tintoretto and « The Last Supper » attributed to Palma il Giovane.

San Paolo. — (*Sestiere di San Polo*). Was apparently founded in '837 by the Doge Pietro Gradonico, and was rebuilt in Gothic style, but has since undergone further alterations. It has a lovely campanile from 1362. It is in the form of a basilica, with three aisles.

On the inside of the facade is Iacopo Tintoretto's « Communion of the Apostles », and « The Baptism of Constantine » by Piazza. On the first altar on the right is « The Virgin Mary and Saints » by Iacopo Tintoretto. In the Chapel of the Most Holy Sacrament, built in Lombardesque style, on the walls are « Episodes from the Life of Christ » (four paintings) by Giuseppe Salviati. In the presbytery is « The Temptation and Liberation of St. Antony », « Conversion of St. Paul », « The Consigning of Keys » and « The Mission of St. Mark »·, all works on canvas by Palma il Giovane, as well as « Glory of the Angels » and « The Way of the Cross » by G.D. Tiepolo. On the high altar is a crucifix painted in the sixteenth century, placed between statues in bronze by Vittoria of « St. Paul » and « St. Antony Abbot ». In the Chapel to the left of the high altar is « The Visitation » by Veronese. In the second altar to the left is « Madonna and St. Giovanni Nepomuceno ».

Redentore. — (*Isola della Giudecca*). This is on the island of Giudecca and was constructed by Pallario in 1577, one of his masterpieces with a beautiful classical facade. The interior has one nave only, with an impressive colonnade going around the walls and giving the impression of solemn majesty. The Presbytery is surmounted by a cupola. On the high Baroque altar, one can admire two bronzes by Girolamo Campagna: « Crucifixion » and « Angel » with symbols of the passion (XVI century). In the sacristy, a beautiful panel by Alvise Vivarini, with « Angel Musicians » and other works by Francesco Bassano and Tintoretto.

San Rocco. *(Campo S. Rocco)* — Renaissance in origin, it was reconstructed in the XVIII century by Scalfarotto with the facade by Bernardo Maccaruzzi.
The interior has one nave and cupola over the Presbytery and includes a series of work by Tintoretto: to the right of the organ, « Annunciation », to the left, « San Rocco presented to the Pope », over the first altar to the right, « San Rocco in the Desert », on the walls of the Presbytery, four super canvases with stories of the Saint: « San Rocco cures the sufferers from the plague, cures the animals, is taken to prison, conforted by an angel ». On the right altar, of the main chapel « Christ bearing the Cross », attributed by some to Giorgione and by others to Titian.

San Salvatore. — *(Mercerie)*. Of very ancient origin it has been many times restored: in the XVI century by Giorgio Spavento, then by Tullio Lombardo and completed by Sansovino and Scamozzi, who placed the lanterns on the three cupolas. The Baroque facade of 1663 is rich in sculpture. The interior with three naves is one of the best examples of Renaissance-Venetian architecture and it contains numerous works of art. Between the second and the third altar of the right nave, sepulchral monument to Doge Francesco Venier, with statues of Charity and Hope, the work of Sansovini. On the third altar, grandiose work by Titian, with the « Annunciation » (1566). On the high altar, altarpiece of chiselled silver, work of Venetian silversmiths of the XIV century; above it a « Transfiguration », by Titian. Chapel to the left of the main one, « Supper at Emmanus », of recent attribution to Giovanni Bellini. In the left transept, monument to the Correr family, by Bernardo Contino.

San Sebastiano. — *(Sestiere di Dorsoduro e Giudecca)*. Church constructed by Francesco Castiglione of Cremona, with the collaboration of Scarpagnino. Restored in 1867, it is full of the art of Paolo Veronese, buried here in 1588.
The interior has one nave and is for the most part ornamented by the works of Paolo Veronese who lavished

Church of San Rocco.

here all the force of his youth, although the building was not suitable for painted decoration, so that the artist had to submit to narrowness of space and bad light. The paintings of the greatest importance are the pictures in the ceiling of the church, with the « Story of Esther »; on the main chapel, « Virgin with Saint Sebastian and other saints », to the left « Martyrdom of Saints Mark and Marcellino », to the right, « Martyrdom of Saint Sebastian » and in the triumphal arch, « Annunciation ». In the chapel to the left of the main one, bust of the artist and in the pavement his tombstone; here is also the organ of which Veronese painted the doors. In the sacristy, with various paintings by his pupils one can admire the five panels on the ceiling, representing the first work of the master executed in Venice. After the third chapel to the Bishop Livio Podocataro, monumental work by Sansovino (1556).

Gli Scalzi (Barefoot Monks). — (*Fondego Scalzi*). Also called church of Santa Maria di Nazareth, formally of the Carmelites, in Baroque style constructed by Longhena (1649), with facade ornamented with many statues by Giuseppe Sardi, (1639). The interior rich with marble,

175

Church of
Santa Maria
di Nazareth,
called " degli
Scalzi ".
It was built
between 1660
and 1689
by Baldassarre
Longhena.
The façade
is the work
of Giuseppe
Sardi.
In the interior,
the tomb
of Lodovico
Manin,
the last Doge
of Venice.

Campo Santo Stefano. The monument in the middle of the square is dedicated to Niccolò Tommaseo and is the work of the sculptor Barzaghi who built it in 1882.

sculpture and elaborate decoration, has only one nave. The ceiling was once frescoed by Tiepolo, with the removal of the Holy House of Loreto, destroyed during the war of 1915-1918, and now replaced by a fresco by the modern painter Ettore Tito (1932). In the second chapel on the right, the vault is frescoed by Tiepolo with « St. Teresa in Glory », as is also the vault of the first chapel on the left, with the « Adoration in the Garden and Angels » (1730). In the second chapel on the left, is buried the last Doge of Venice, Ludovico Manin.

Santo Stefano. — *(Campo S. Stefano)*. Romanesque-Gothic church of the end of the XIII century and many times restored. It has a brick facade doorways in flowery Gothic, by the brothers Bon. The characteristic interior has three naves divided by two rows of columns in Greek and red Veronese marble and ribbed ceiling. Here are valuable works of art, amongst which, in the chapel in the end of the right nave, « St. Vitellius and Saints » by Vittore Carpaccio (1514) and in the sacristy, three works by Tintoretto, with the « Last Supper », « Washing of the Feet », and « Christ in the

179

Campo San Trovaso.

Garden »; by Bartolomeo Vivarini, polyptych with « St. Peter and St. Lawrence » by Piazzetta, the « Archangel Raphael and Saints »; and by Palma the Elder, « Virgin and Saints ». In the presbytery, with a great polygonal apse, magnificent Gothic choir of the XV century. The bell tower leans more than another in the city.

San Trovaso. — (*Sestiere di Dorsoduro*). Is the church of the Saints Gervasio and Protasio, and was already in existence in the eleventh century, but reconstructed after a fire in the classic Palladian style (1583). The lovely interior consists of one nave, a large presbytery and side chapels. On the third altar on the right is « San Francesco di Paola, Faith and Charity » by Alvise di Friso, and on the same wall is a work from the school of Giovanni Bellini: « Madonna and Child ». In the right transept notice the beautiful altar frontal, a Renaissance bas-relief, perhaps by Pietro Lombardo which portrays « Angels with the symbols of the Passion ». Also on the right, in the chapel next to the high altar is a « Crucifixion » by Domenico Tintoretto, on the altar, and on the wall is a masterpiece by Jacobello del Fiore: « St. Crisogono on horseback », which is attributed by some to Michele Giambono. In the Presbytery is « The Epiphany » and « St. Joachim cast out the temple » by Iacopo Tintoretto and pupils. In the chapel on the left of the high altar is « The Temptation of St. Antony » by Iacopo Tintoretto; in the Sacristy « Madonna » by Rosalba Carriera and « St. John and Mary Magdalene », which is attributed Tintoretto. In the Chapel of the Holy Sacrament, which is in the left transept, are « The Last Supper » and « The Washing of the feet » by Tintoretto, and above the nearby altar is « Deposition » by Palma il Giovane, and by the same artist is « Nativity », in the third altar on the left.

S ZULIAN

THE VENETIAN « SCHOOLS »

The Schools were actually religious corporations, almost all founded towards the middle of the thirteenth century, by the Dominicans and the Franciscans, with the aim of assisting the foor, and their contribution was invaluable during wars and plagues. The bequests of benefactors were such that these « Schools » were able to construct beautiful buildings and enrich their artistic patrimony. Unfortunately political events led to their being suppressed, and the works of art accumulated during the course of centuries were dispersed into various different museums. The only « School » which still exists and functions that is of San Rocco. We will quote here in alphabetical order the names of these Schools with details of the art works.

Scuola degli Albanesi. — (*In Calle del Piovan, Sestiere di S. Marco*). Beautiful facade in Lombardesque stlye (1531) with bas-reliefs representing the « Madonna and Child », « San Gallo » and « St. Maurice » Above the « Sultan Mahomet observing the castle of Scutari ».

Scuola dell'Angelo Custode. — (*Campo dei SS. Apostoli, Sesitere Cannaregio*).
Facade in the classic style, constructed by Andrea Tirali; in the interior (now the Chiesa Evangelica) two valuable works « Madonna in glory and the Archangel Raphael » by Sebastiano Ricci, and a « Christ » in the act of benediction, by an artist of the school of Titian.

Scuola dei Battiloro. — (*next to the Church of St. Stae or St. Eustace, Sestiere di S. Croce*).
This facade of 1711 constitutes one of the most beautiful Venetian rococò buildings.

Scuola dei Calegheri. — (*Campo S. Tomà, Sestiere di S. Polo*).
Used to belong to the shoe-makers. It has a lovely ogival portal, a bas relief attributed to Pietro Lombardo « St. Mark curing the shoemaker Aniano » and the relief « Madonna of Misericordia) which dates back to the fifteenth century.

Scuola Grande dei Carmini. — (*On the Campo S. Margherita is the Calle della Scuola, Sestiere di Dorsoduro*).
A graceful building of the seventeenth century attributed to Baldassarre Longhena (1668). In the room on the ground floor on the altar is a « Virgin Mary » by S. Piatti, and on the walls are great canvases by N. Bambini: «'The Flight into Egypt », « The Assunmption », « The Birth of Mary », and « The Circumcision ». In the hall on the first floor, besides other works by minor artists, is the great ceiling composed of nine paintings which G.B. Tiepolo painted beteween 1739 and 1744, when his style had reached full maturity. In the centre « The Madonna of the Carmelites giving the scapular to Blessed Simon Stock » and around are « Virtues and angels flying around ». Notice the grace and luminosity of the central painting. In the room of the Albergo the « Virgin Mary » on the ceiling is by Padovanino, and on the walls are episodes from the New Testament by the arstis A. Balestra. In a passage leading to the Room of the Archives is « Judith and Holoferne », a masterpiece by G.B. Piazzetta, and in the room itself are some interesting works by minor artists.

Scuola Grande di S. Marco. — (*Campo S. Giovanni e Paolo, Sestiere di Castello*).
This is now the Civil Hospital. The School was founded in 1437, but when it was destroyed by a fire it was rebuilt by Pietro Lombardo and Mauro Codussi betwenn 1485 and 1495. The facade can be considered a masterpiece of Venetian Renaissance architecture. The statues are the work of B. Bon and T. Lombardo, the former of whom did the « St. Mark and brothers » and the « Charity », the latter the bas-reliefs « Baptism and Cure of Aniano ». On the first floor in the Salone del Capitolo is a beautiful sixteenth century ceiling in wood, while the altar is of the school of Sansovino. From here one enters the Sala dell'Albergo, the ceiling of which is wooden, decorated in gold and silver, the work of Pietro and Biagio da Faenza. On the walls are paintings by Palma il Giovane, Giovanni Mansueti and Vittore Belliniano, and the libraries contain texts from the Medica Library.

Rio dei Mendicanti and the Civil Hospital.

Scuola di San Giovanni Evangelista. — (*Campo S. Stin, Sestiere di San Polo*). This was originally a hospice founded in 1261 by the Badoer family but in 1340 it became the seat of the Confraternity of the Battuti, whose Patron was St. John the Evengelist. It is an architectural masterpiece of the Venetian Renaissance (1454); the courtyard is by Pietro Lombardo (1481), and the lovely portal was designed in 1512 by Mauro Codussi, who also designed the spacious salon. On the upper floor the large hall contains an altar by G. Massari (1730) who also transformed the hall into the style of the eighteenth century. On the altar is a statue of St. John by Morlaiter, and the stories of the Saint are painted by Marieschi and Guarana. On the ceiling is « The Struggle of Christ with the Anti-Christ » by G. Angeli, and the figures on the sides are by G. Diziani. Towards the altar are further paintings: on side « St. John » by Marieschi, and on the other the seven Angels and seven vases in octagonal frames are the work of J. Guarama, and the « Scenes from the Apocalypse » are by Domenico Tiepolo. On the walls to the right of the door are « The Transfiguration » and « The Collapse of the Temple of Diana » by Domenico Tintoretto. In the room of .the Cross there is a beautiful Reliquary of the Cross, and on the ceiling « The Triumph of the Cross » by F. Maggiotto. On the walls of the Albergo are four stories of the Apocalypse by Palma il Giovane, and in the room of the Archives the ornate ceiling is frescoed by Guarana.

Scuola di San Rocco. — (*Campo S. Rocco, Sestiere di S. Polo*). Bartolommeo Bon il Giovane inaugurated the construction in 1517 of this building for the Confraternity of S. Rocco; Sante Lombardo continued it and it was finished in 1549 by Antonio Scarpagnino. The Scuola Grande di San Rocco is the one best known by the tourists because of the magnificent cycle of paintings by Iacopo Tintoretto. Before entering do not overlook the facade by Scarpagnino, made up of two orders, with mullioned windows, below, and a tympanum on balusters above, beautifully decorated with multi-coloured marbles, bas-reliefs and a magnificent portal. In order to look at the numerous paintings in chronological order one should enter the large hall on the ground foor, which we will look at on the way back, and climb to the first floor, entering the Sala dell'Albergo. Tintoretto began the decoration of this room in 1564: on the ceiling is « San Rocco in glory », on the wall the grandiose « Crucifixion » and around the room from the right: « Christ at Calvary », two figures of the Prophets, « Jesus before Pilate » and « Jesus crowned with thorns ». On an easel is « Christ bearing the Cross » which the critics attribute either to Giorgione or Titian. Now we pass into the magnificent rectangular salon, where beside the door on the left is a « Self-portrait » by Tintoretto, who was then 66. In the ceiling . of gilded intaglio, divided into sections, are 21 paintings by Tintoretto. The best place to look at them is from the centre at the end of the room, looking towards the altar: « Adam and Eve », « Moses parting the waters », on the left « God appearing to Moses », on the right « The Crossing of the Red Sea », « Jonah coming out of the stomach of the whale », « The chastisement of the serpents », to the left « The Vision of Ezechiel », to the right « An episode from the life of Jacob », « The sacrifice of Isaac », « The falling of manna », to the left « Elias and the Angel », to the right « Elisha distributing the bread » « The Passover », on the altar « Glory of St. Rocco ». Along the sides are « Annunciation » by Titian and « The Visitation » by Tintoretto.

Now return to the end wall, and we will look around from left to right: « San Rocco », « St. Sebastian », « The Crib », « The

Lido of Venice.

Baptism of Christ »; « The Resurrection », « The Sermon in the
Orchard », « The Last Supper »; now cross to the other side,
passing in front of the altar, « The Multiplication of the loaves »,
« The Resurrection of Lazarus », « The Ascension », « The Piscina
Probatica » and « Christ and Satan ». After the altar is the Sala
della Cancelleria, on the walls of which are an « Ecce Homo »
attributed to Titian, and a « San Rocco » by Bernardo Strozzi.
On the stucco ceiling is « The Glory of St. Rocco » by G. Angeli.
Turning back, we descend the large staircase, on the walls of
which are two large paintings of the seventeenth century by A.
Zanchi and Pietro Negri, and enter the large ground floor room,
which is very impressive with the space divided by two rows
of Corinthian columns into three aisles; along the walls are beautiful mullioned windows, and there is a beam roof. Around the
walls are eight great paintings by Tintoretto, done between
1583 and 1587.

MURANO - Apse of the Basilica of Santa Maria and Donato. It dates back to the seventh century but was rebuilt in Venetian-Byzantine style of the twelfth century.

VENICE LIDO

It is one of the most famous and elegant bathing place in Italy, situated 4 Km. from Venice and extending for about 12 Km.

500 metres from the Lido, (connected by a special steamer), is the *island of San Lazzaro degli Armeni*, quiet and solitary, occupied by a college of Armenian Mekhitarist Fathers, which boasts a library and a gallery of painting with works by Tiepolo, Guardi, Andrea del Sarto, Quercino, etc.

MURANO

1,2 Km. from Venice. It is a typical lagoon centre situated on five islands, and is famous for its glass manufacturing industry that goes back to the XIII century. In the Giustinian Palace, is the MUSEUM OF ARTE VETRARIA (Glass Museum) where one may admire the best examples of glass from the XIV to the XVIII centuries: Roman and Egyptian glass, and foreign productions.

MURANO - Above: **The Grand Canal;**
below: **a picturesque view of the island.**

TORCELLO - A detail of this beautiful island
taken from the landing-place.

Saints Mary and Donato

Church of the VII century, re-constructed in the XII century. It is Venetian-byzantine with single hexagonal apse, with two orders of arcades decorated by graceful niches and loggias. The basical interior has three naves divided by ten marble columns with stupendous Corinthian capitals. The pavement mosaic is of the XII century. At the beginning of the left wall the large wooden anchor inrelief with paintings (St Donato) is of the XIV century and constitutes an example of an ancient XIV century Venetian art form. The mosaic in the apse vaults with golden background, depicts the *Virgin in Adoration* and is of the XII century.

TORCELLO

10 Km. from Venice, it is one of the most fascinating places. Lonely village on a little island, it was once a flourishing centre of life and comerce, but with the increase in the power of Venice, Torcello fell into decadence and there remains only the memory of its monuments.

Cathedral
Dedicated to Santa Maria Assunta, its origin is said to go back to 639 and it was re-constructed in the beginning of the XI century, together with the majestic bell

tower. In front of the facade, the remains of the Baptistery of the VIII century, with circular plan.

The austere and simple interior has three naves divided by columns. The inside wall of the facade is completely covered with a Byzantine mosaic of the XII and XIII centuries depicting the *Last Judgement*.

Santa Fosca

The origins of the church go back to the XI century. The external plan is octagonal in form and surrounded, on five sides, by a portico with arched buttresses on capitals. Of the three apses, the central one has two orders of arcades. The interior has the form of a Greek cross with columns and Byzantine capitals; on the altar wooden statue of *St. Fosca*, XV century.

Finito di stampare nel Marzo 1976
dalle Arti Grafiche Parigi & Maggiorelli – Firenze